SO-ANX-372

Legal Almanac Series No. 23

RELIGION, CULTS AND THE LAW

REVISED SECOND EDITION

by Abraham Burstein

*This Legal Almanac has been revised
by the Oceana Editorial Staff*

Irving J. Sloan
General Editor

1980
OCEANA PUBLICATIONS, INC.
Dobbs Ferry, New York

Library of Congress Cataloging in Publication Data

Burstein, Abraham
    Religion, cults and the law
    (Legal almanac series; no. 23)

ISBN: 0-379-11133-0

©Copyright 1980 by Oceana Publications, Inc.

All rights reserved. No part of this publication may be reproduced or transmitted in any form or by any means, electronic or mechanical, including photocopy, recording, xerography, or any information storage and retrieval system, without permission in writing from the publisher.

Manufactured in the United States of America

TABLE OF CONTENTS

Chapter 1

LAWS CONCERNING RELIGION

The Religious Society

With very few exceptions, every state welcomes the *incorporation* of organizations with religious aims. No mere individuals, however, may claim such rom the state. A Society or church property must be a group affair. As a group it obtains property, is accorded tax and other exemptions, and carries on the many activities, social, charitable, and educational, which have always supplemented its activities of public worship.

There is no legal objection to any householder conducting worship in his own home or other location not specifically assigned for religious services, provided there is no infringement upon the rights and comfort of other individuals or the public.

Most states prohibit location of liquor stores or other businesses not in complete public favor, within a specified distance from a church or synagogue.

Like any other corporation, a religious society does not necessarily have perpetual existence. It is possible for a religious society, whose authorities so provide, to *dissolve* by mere agreement of its members. Or where it has limited its incorporation for a fixed period, it will automatically cease at expiration of that time.

It is always possible that a religious society will abandon the aims for which it came into being, and cease exercising the functions regularly pacticed by it; it can then be regarded as dissolved without further legal act. Disposition of property, if any, must be entrusted to the judgment of the courts.

From a variety of decisions accepted by all state courts, certain principles affecting *consolidations* of church groups become evident. As corporations generally obtain the power to consolidate only through consent and authority of the legislatures, the same procedure is imposed upon religious corporations. By extension, even the *merger* of unincorporated religious societies generally requires that legislative sanction.

But there are certain obstacles to merger even where both bodies at first appear altogether willing to affect them. If there is anytthing in the fundamental law of either institution expressly or implicitly forbidding such action, it will not be sanctioned. Likewise, if there are differences in faith, there must be express provisions for altering the confession. And if the original endowment restricts the group to a particular faith, it cannot be allowed to renounce that the faith or join with another organization not professing its own religious principles.

Most of the state codes contain no specific statutes for church mergers and dissolutions; some mention only the matter of consolidation, and some only that of dissolving religious corporations. There are sufficient provisions for these changes in the general statutes. In any event, such projects demand the intervention of lawyers and courts of law, hence exact details need wait upon the event.

Ordinarily those persons who qualify to be *members* of a religious society do so according to the constitution or by-laws of the society. Submission to constituted authority and profession of faith are ordinarily treated by the law as inherent in membership.

Any *constitution* adopted by the members of such a group will be given legal recognition unless its provisions are unreasonable or in conflict with the law. The same applies to by-laws adopted pursuant to such constitution. Ordinarily, the constitution may be changed in regard to fundamental matters of faith only by unanimous consent of the membership.

The law will recognize any procedure for *meetings* or *elections* which the rules of the society provide or which is established by its customs, but will give relief from instances of gross irregularilty. In the absence of any rule or custom, parliamentary procedure will be assumed as a standard.

Since a religious corporation, theortically and in accord with the common law, has unrestricted control over its possessions and can *dispose* of them in the same manner as other corporations, it would seem that this privilege should not be abridged in actual practice. But everywhere in this country there are statutes which require sanction of the appropriate court before a church property may be transferred or encumbered. When the court so orders, there are generally added directions concerning disposition of proceeds of a sale or other change in form of ownership.

Often the court order requires that a church that is sold be conveyed to a group professing the same creed, or of the same denomination; but there are numerous cases of a church being sold to a synagogue group, or vice versa.

Under most statutes covering such transfers, a majority vote among members or pewholders is not considered sufficient authorization for the religious corporation to complete the sale, nor to impel the court to sanction it.

It has generally been held that a church site and structure may be sold to pay the salary of the pastor, although in one state this method of satisfying a judgment against the church was held to be unlawful.

An incorporated religious society is permitted to carry on a variety of secular activities. It may not derive income from any worldly business, but may do so from the property it owns and which is employed for religious purposes. Otherwise, it must rely upon voluntary dues and contributions.

The rule applies in all cases, no matter how urgent be the immediate needs of the group. The religious society is forbidden to rent a farm, in order to grow a profitable crop thereon; to lease a store, for the purpose of renting out horses and carriages; or to hire a vessel for paid water transportation of passengers.

If the society contracts for a steamboat excursion to raise money for itws maintenance, it does so without a legal right - although this and similar methods of church fund-raising are common, as everyone knows.

Only to the extent that secular activities are part of its doctrine and mode of religious observance may they be carried on by incorporated religious societies. Such societies have been forbidden to build structures for rental purposes, or purchase real estate for speculation.

Other prohibitions have been against conducting a commercial printery, transporting passengers for hire, conducting a savings bank business.

In no case can the society go beyond the purposes set out in its chapter. A case in point is a corporation proposing to supply preachers with literature, which tried to branch out into establishing an orphans' home.

Where specific occupations are prohibited under court decisions the prohibitions holds even though every dollar gained in profit is devoted to the purposes of the religious corporation.

Unless a member acts to incur or ratify a debt of the society, or is bound by the laws of the society to anwer for its *liabilities*, he has no obligation in respect to such matters. But he is liable for assessments by the society upon its members in accordance with the rules of the society.

The religious society is the group attending devine services. The *corporation* is the owner and manager of the properties, with a theoretical permanent existence. A member of one is not necessarily a part of the other.

Two religious corporations may not *merge* and yet continue separate activities. Consolidation must be complete, and there must be collective unity of property and external relations.

A religious body may sue to prevent use of a misleading name by a newly formed religious group. If the first body is in any way harmed or confused because of such action, it can request legal relief like any legal corporation.

The Clergy

Courts will adjudicate issues involving the rights of clergymen to their positions. If contractual or property rights are at issue, the courts will take jurisdiction. if, however, questions involving exercise of ecclesiastical authority are at issue, the courts will not ordinarily intervene.

In a number of states clergymen suffer disabilities because of their official position. In a number of states they are excluded from election to the legislature or other high state offices. While this was once the norm in southern states, only Maryland and Tennessee still forbid public office to clergymen. Some states do not permit clergymen to draw and witness wills on the ground of possible undue influence.

Ministers are as a rule exempt from jury and other local civic duties and obligations. Some states in the east exempt retired ministers from taxation. The federal income tax exempts the rental value of a home provided for the minister by his congregation. No minister or theological student need accept drafting into the armed forces.

Religious workers may not interfere in the work of social agencies handling public charges.

Generally, statements of the clergy in church or synagogue are privileged in regard to slander or other suits. A pastor is not liable if he merely carries out a policy of church discipline, and from his pulpit reads a valid excommunication promulgated by a church tribunal. Only if he goes on to make personal charges, to advise his congregation to avoid the excommunicate and have no personal or business dealings with him, may the clergyman be held for defamation of character.

Except that he need not divulge religiously received confessions, no minister is ever above the law. He may be punished for any crime as the law prescribes. He may be sued for damages in such cases as assult, libel, alienation of affection, or other acts in which a tort is committed. Nor is a clergyman privileged to employ slander or obscene language in rebuking sin, or use undue force in ejecting a person lawfully in the room of worship with him.

The Family

The law wishes to assure the validity of marriages, since that relationship is fraught with so many important consequences for both individual and state.

Complications at the best disturbing, and at worst socially disrupting, may arise from solemnization of marriages by persons not legally recognized as qualified to do so. Hence the law requires that every clergyman of every faith, and every public official so privileged, must receive official sanction before being permitted to perform a marriage ceremony.

Most generally, the clergyman must submit a public registration and then be formally licensed to serve as officiating minister. He must identify himself before the proper official, and furnish proof of his qualifications and of his status in his religious denomination.

Although all states provide that clergymen are empowered to perform nuptials, they must have some proof of ordination. Nevertheless, in New York and elsewhere the statutes are so worded that a person who can prove that he is conducting the spiritual activities of a functioning house of worship is held to be a full-fledged clergyman and can preside at a marriage. A number of states require that the celebrant be "settled" in the work of the ministry.

Efforts have been made by legislatures to limit the clergyman qualified to solemnize marriages to those affiliated with a religion listed in the most recent federal census of religious bodies. But such laws have been held invalid. The status of a clergyman is not dependent upon any official listing, but upon his bona fide religious service to a religious institution, and as a rule with proof of actual ordination.

Where the ceremony is performed by one not authorized to do so it is ordinarily considered void. Decisions in a number of jurisdictions have proclaimed that if either party believes the celebrant to be so authorized, the marriage remains valid.

Where a religious ceremony is required to validate a marriage, it has been held that where it is solemnized by one apparently an ordained minister even though he be actually unqualified, the marriage is to be considered legal.

In those states permitting common law marriage, obviously a ceremony solemnized by an unauthorized person will achieve validity through the very fact of the consorting of the parties.

Licenses are everywhere prescribed before a marriage may be solemnized. In California, West Virginia, and Wyoming, decisions have held that the license is always mandatory, and that a marriage performed without it is void. But the general rule is that statutes prescribing licenses are merely directory, and do not destroy the validity of a marriage contracted without fulfillment of these statutory provisions, but a clergyman renders himself liable to criminal prosecution for failure to require production of the prescribed marriage license.

In common law marriage, it seems that almost every violation of law, including that of serological tests, can be condoned, and the marriage be considered legal. But generally it is required that a third party has heard the joint profession of the man and woman.

It is a general rule that if a wedding has been solemnized by a clerk or judge so empowered, and the parties later wish to go through a religious ceremony, no additional license is required. This generally applies even when the second ceremony is held in another state.

State statutes do not ordinarily prescribe an exact form of ceremony. Any form of ceremony set up by the law and custom of various denominations and religious societies is authorized and accepted by the law. Either a religious or civil ceremony is sufficient except that in Delaware, Maryland and West Virginia a religious ceremony is required by statute.

At common law, differences in race or faith have no bearing on the right to be married. There is no statute anywhere in the United States forbidding marriage of persons of different religions. Of course such statutes would be clearly unconstitutional.

A visiting performer of a marriage may or may not have to be registered in the state where he performs the marriage. Custom rather than law governs this question. Thus, while New Jersey requires no registration of any kind for a clergyman from another state who wishes to perform a ceremony in that state, every visiting clergyman on a similar task in New York City is expected to sign a registration book. There is no case, however, of a marriage performed by a visiting clergyman fully licensed in his own state, being legally invalidated.

The law sanctions all forms of marriage solemnization in accord with the laws and customs of existing sects and societies.

Indians have never been forbidden marriage in keeping with their tribunal customs. Quakers, Mormons, Christian Scientists, and others who have no clergymen in the accepted sense of the term, but leaders, readers, and others thus

7

differently designated, may still perform ceremonies that will not be adjudged illegal.

The Amish, who object to giving oath, need not answer questions on license applications under oath, but their bishop may attest the truth of their statements. In short, the states offer every opportunity for legitimate sects to carry on their customs and traditions in the matter of marriage performance.

An *ante-nuptial agreement* concerning *religious training of children* is not inviolable. Quite to the contrary, No father can divest himself of custody of his children in any respect, and he need not follow any agreement made with his wife before her death concerning their religious training. He has the right to change their forms of religious instruction. The same applies to the mother.

In cases where relatives insist upon guardians of orphans who will train them in the agreed religion, the religious considerations do not prevail, but only the well-being of the children.

In all cases *divorce* is a matter of civil law, therefore a state court will not adjudge validity of marriage and adjudge divorce on the basis of the religious law of the parties. A Mormon divorce by mutual consent was adjudged invalid. Rabbinical divorces have no validity without normal judicial proceedings under state law.

As indicated earlier, each party to a marriage has full right to his or her unique and religious practices.

Where religious differences are not mere ideas, but are conducive to actions harmful or oppressive to the spouse, there may possibly be valid grounds for seeking a divorce. Thus, serpent worshipers who wind poisonous snakes about their necks, or practitioners of the bizarre arts of voodoo, or members of some sects that inflict bodily harm on their devotees in the frenzies of worship, can cause actual physical injury to their spouses--and from such contingencies they undoubtedly can obtain legal redress. Even ridiculing the other's church is not sufficient reason for legally enforced separation.

But when one party compels the other to comply with his religion, despite the other's utter aversion thereto, relief may be

8

granted. This is also the case where one party develops a great and sudden interest in propagating another religion, and to this end neglects his family. In one case the husband of a religious healer was granted a divorce on the ground that his wife's conduct had seriously injured his health and reason.

In some states refusal to cohabitat on religious grounds is not considered legal cruelty and thus grounds for divorce. This applies to wives who proclaim that they have formed mystical other-worldly marriages.

But California, Michigan, New Hampshire, Oregon, and Washington consider such refusal valid grounds for divorce, no matter what reasons be given. In New Hampshire six months' connection with a religious society forbidding cohabitation is sufficient to warrant relief by divorce; in Kentucky, the membership must last five years.

As opposed to old English law, which gives the father prior rights, American courts have posited the doctrine of equality in determining the form of *religious instruction for children* when both are living, and exclusive rights thereto for the survivor.

The courts will not intervene in a domestic quarrel as religious training of a couple's children, but the conflict must not raise actual questions of the welfare of the offspring must remain within the home.

Religion is not the primary consideration in awarding *custody of a child*. The welfare of the child is primary, although for many reasons every effort is made to assure conformity of faith between guardian and ward. Natural ties are to be considered as well as character and feelings of the contending parties. Age, health, sex, surroundings and physical and cultural needs all coupled with pecuniary advantages, are other criteria. However, even a father may be deprived of the guardianship of his child if he professes a belief in a sect adjudged obnoxious to society.

Ordinarily, courts attempt to place young wards in institutions providing for instruction in their parental faith. This is of course possible where the faiths have established institutions for children of their own persuasion. But the fundamental rule is that when children become public charges the state assumes the role of parents and may - theoretically - direct the kind of religious instruction to be given. This means that the state can arbitrarily determine the religion of children of unknown parentage. It is the general pattern for the state and local jurisdictions to divide foundlings in regular order into Protestants and Catholics, and they are so reared by the institutions established by these churches for that purpose. However, this procedure is bound to be challenged in the foreseeable future, and just what alternatives will arise can hardly be predicted.

The question not infrequently is raised as to whether a parent may refuse to call a physician for an ailing child, on the ground of his belief in faith healing. Any parent who refuses to employ proper medical attention for a sick child can be prosecuted criminally if the child dies as the result of such neglect. No claim of religious belief may stand in the way of the welfare and life of a minor. Prayer is not in itself a remedy, and recourse to prayer alone in an emergency of this sort is inconsistent with the peace and security of the state.

Liabilities, Immunities, Privileges, and Protections

Legal limitations may be placed upon the use or ownership of property by religious societies. But any such limitation, whether by constitution of statute, may be imposed in the public interest; it cannot be imposed to hinder the free exercise of religion. The provisions of a will or trust with regard to such matters will be given effect by the law.

Although some state constitutions are silent concerning the matter of exemption from *taxation* for church property, and others delegate such powers to the legislature as the case may arise, in the main such property pays no assessments.

It is made clear, however, that land not actually occupied by the church society, nor necessary for its purposes within reason, nor actually employed for church purpose, will not be exempted.

There are few variations in the wording of the statutes. The Florida constitution specifies that the property must be in fact "owned" by the society; Idaho uses the phrase, "belonging to"; in Nebraska it must be "owned and used"." Iowa limits the size of the land exempted- it may not exceed 320 acres.

A number of state decisions have stated that taxes are not to be confused with special assessments, as a general thing. The latter are not taxes within constitutional provisions of exemption. On the other hand, several states including Arkansas, Georgia, Illinois, Indiana, Maryland, Michigan, Missouri, Ohio, and Pennsylvania have established that tax exemptions of property religiously used do not include special assessments.

Many states have no constitutional or statutory provisions specifically covering the question of taxing church-owned cemeteries. On the whole, taxation of burial grounds belonging to religious societies is not probable.

In the matter of *church-leased property* most state codes have no provisions. Judicial construction remains vague and, on the basis of any study of constitution and statutes, can only be decided as to probability or lack of probability of such taxation.

Definite prohibition of such tax exemption is found in the laws of Arizona, California, and Ohio. But similar prohibitions may be derived from the wording of some state laws. Thus, Indiana, Nevada, North Carolina, Oregon, South Carolina, Tennessee, and Vermont all which employ the word "owned," implying that mere leasing to a church organization is not sufficient to warrant exemption. In New Jersey the word is "owns," in South Dakota, "belonging to." In Pennsylvania "legal or equitable title" is required.

In most cases the probabilities are that such church-leased lands will be exempted from taxation by the authorities. In this regard many states stress the "use" of the land as the determining factor. Among such states are Arkansas, Florida, Georgia, Illinois, Kentucky, Maryland, Montana, New Hampshire, New Mexico, North Dakota, Rhode Island, Utah, Washington, West Virginia, and Wyoming.

States in which exemption is unlikely are, in addition to those requiring actual church ownership as indicated earlier, are Iowa, Maine, Massachusets, and Mississippi.

Although some state codes carry no provisions concerning *taxation of a residence* owned by a church but used as the home of its minister or rabbi, the general trend has been not to exempt such structures from taxation. Where such exemption is provided by statute, the use of the house must be immediate and continued. Incidental use, or mere ownership by a church or closeness to the church, is not sufficient. There is no exemption in the states of Georgia, Illinois, Indiana, Kansas, Kentucky, Louisiana, Minnesota, Montana, Missouri, Ohio, Pennsylvania, and Texas. Definite exemptions has been established in Michigan, Rhode Island, South Carolina, Washington, West Virginia, and Wisconsin.

Colorado and New York grant *exemption* if the value is not over $3,000; Massachusetts and New Jersey when not over $5,000; and Maine, when not over $6,000.

While specific laws are absent from the codes, generally a lot on which church property is being erected is at once exempted. Arkansas specifies that a vacant lot owned by a religious society is taxable. Florida, Maine Maryland, and New Jersey insist upon actual use.

In any case of an unincorporated religious society, members of the organization instrumental in incurring *liabilities* for it are themselves liable therefore. Any person who authorizes or ratifies transactions of the society or those made in its name is responsible unless it is agreed between the parties to the contract that such person shall not be individually liable on the contract. On the other hand, those who in no manner participate in such transactions are relieved of all liability.

The principle here involved is that of one acting as agent for a society without legal status of existence. The individual, committee, or board involved can, if conditions warrant, be held responsible for all contracts entered into. However, the same principle has been invoked on occasion against boards of trustees of incorporated religious societies, who are charged with individual liability on contracts executed by them as trustees.

Where no such express provision exists, a church officer cannot be held liable for the contracts entered into by his predecessor.

The *remedy* of a member who is improperly excluded from the use of church facilities is to take legal action in court to vindicate his rights. If he acts by way of self-help involving trespass, he incurs liability as a trespasser though his legal right to admission is ultimately recognized in court.

There is a division among the states in the question of church *liability for negligence*. Some follow the rule applied to charitable organizations and exempt religious groups from such liability, while others treat religious societies as any other non-charitable group would be treated. In those jurisdictions where there is exemption from liability, it extends to all the property used by the religious society for its various avowed purposes, such as a business conducted to supply funds for the society.

A *clergyman's* profession requires that his *character* be without stain, therefore reflections on his character often cause more harm than similar statements or writings about a lay citizen. Words employed about a minister may be actionable when they are not actionable applied to the layman.

Among accusations against clergymen that have been held libelous or slanderous by the courts are--charges of disobedience to church law, violation of the Commandment against using the name of the Lord in vain, untruthfulness, drunkenness, insanity, and immorality.

Such charges are actionable even though the accused minister be not clerically engaged at the time they are made.

But when a clergyman enters politics, the distinction in these regards between himself and laymen no longer holds. He must suffer all criticism ensuing from free discussion of public questions, and must expect an equal probability of being brought into public ridicule or contempt.

If a clergyman becomes a paid lobbyist, he may be called such without fear on the part of his assailant.

Denouncing a religion is not a form of personal *libel*. If, however, a person is charged with infidility to his faith, or with being hypocritical or irreverent, or with having been expelled from his church, or is otherwise directly and by name attacked on grounds of religion, he may seek legal redress.

Laws against *blasphemy* are being removed from statute books, and where they exist they are seldom enforced. Although the offense has been defined as "maliciously reviling

God and religion," in point of fact only assults on Christianity and Christian doctrines have been held actionable.

Prosecution for blasphemy is not undertaken "to prevent or restrain the formation of any opinions or the profession of any religious sentiments whatever, but to restrain and punish acts which have a tendency to disturb the public peace," held a Massachusetts court.

In all states blatant blasphemy or profanity may be punished on grounds of breaches of peace or disorderly conduct. For such is generally the nature of the offender's conduct. However, sixteen states still provide specific penalties for the original crime.

Public monies to aid religious societies are generally prohibited by state constitutions. Thus land grants for the benefit of religion cannot be voted. Even for charity and education, no state funds may be placed under sectarian control. No contract may be made by a political subdivision with an ecclasiastical body that receives full pay for public service rendered.

A church may *erect a religious institution* on state property for the use of inmates of a public institution. The state looses nothing; the religious group gains nothing for itself. As the atheist has the right to act according to his lack of belief, he at the same time cannot prevent others from observing their religion.

Licensing of outdoor or street meetings apply to religious groups. Public streets and square are not considered set apart for purposes of worship. For outdoor meetings and parades licenses must be obtained as for outdoor gatherings of any other kind.

Religious groups are granted exemption from prohibition laws if they require wines for religious purposes. This has been the practice of both federal and state statutes.

Many persons have sought to defend frauds on the ground that the law's interference with their crimes is a denial of religious liberty of the expression of religious preferences.

Phrenologists, palmists, astrologers, and various miracle workers, have sought defense under religious pretenses, but the law has never accepted that subterfuge.

14

In an attempt to destroy the kosher laws of New York States, an appellant to the Supreme Court tried to defend his violations on the basis of his own religious ideas. But it was obvious to the court that the fraud was being perpetrated under sham protection of the Constitution.

This topsy-turvey reasoning has never succeeded with the courts. In one case the court declared that "this modern attempt to excuse violations of lawful salutary police regulations, enacted for the protection of the community, by appeals to constitutional rights and religious beliefs, does not find favor with the courts."

Fortune-tellers have often claimed ordination in a religious society. Spiritualists, too, are generally held guilty of a kind of fortune-telling, but on occasion have been acquitted of any crime.

In every case, the state may prevent "free exercise" of a real or purported religion when the customs and observances and methods of a sect are adjudged nuisances, infringements of the rights of others, or threats to the welfare of the community.

In every case where regulations have been established within a church body concerning *expulsion or excommunication of a member*, these rules are binding upon every member, who is presumed to have accepted them together with his membership.

Where, however, no set rules have been established, the common law must prevail. That is, notice must be served on the member, and every opportunity be given to reply to all charges on defense. If this is not done, the expulsion is illegal and without force.

If a member has been wrongfully expelled from an unincorporated association, no legal writ will be issued to compel his reinstatement unless by the law of the society, membership therein carries with it the right to share individually in the joint property of the society, or some other civil or property right, distinct from and in addition to the mere right of fellowship in the spiritual or ecclesiastical body.

Such a writ of mandamus is always held legally proper where the expulsion has been ordered by an incorporated body. But even so, most courts observe the general rule that there will be no interference with church discipline or expulsion of members unless injury is done to the expellee's civil or property rights.

All the above statements are subject to varying decisions in the courts of specific states. In Massachusetts and nebraska courts have refused to accept as final a church tribunal's expulsion of a member where the member has not been notified of the charges against him or given the opportunity to be heard in his defense. As a rule, however, the church judgment is not interferred with by the courts, no matter what accusation be made as to its lack of regularity.

It is always possible that a church organization be headed by dishonest men who will seek to expel dissident members in order to carry out some fraudulent scheme to take control of, misappropriate, or misuse church property. In such a case, since this is a matter of public dishonesty, the civil courts have full jurisdiction to review the illegal action of the controlling officials.

The Supreme Court has held that a person traveling about selling or distributing religious tracts is exempted from *licensing requirements*. The court considered these activities a legitimate method of spreading religious beliefs.

In every state disturbing public worship is punishable, with special laws concerning this kind of disorderly conduct applied in nearly all. Fines extending as high as $500 are levied for this misdemeanor, although as a rule they are $100 or below. Prison sentences, ranging from two days to six months, may be meted out.

The state will never permit religious worship to be left to the mercy of a mob, or be molested in any way. Every member of the assembly is individually entitled to protection.

Under the law the clergyman is entitled to protection from molestation, and by extension even the taker of the collection. The disturbances must be willful and intentional to warrant conviction. Making loud noises in the vicinity of the church, mugging at the windows, and similar conduct, are actionable.

Members of the congregation may also be prosecuted for disturbing worship. Talking out of turn, creating laughter and mockery, starting a quarrel, and other unseemly conduct are punished; but a member who calls attention to a pastor's deviation from accepted church doctrine is not. Any person abused at a service may properly defend himself.

Sufficient force used to remove a disturber is not an assult.

These forms of legal protection apply only if the meeting has been called for religious worship. Only the ordinary rights of protection are to be accorded business, musical, or other non-religious gatherings of the group.

Specific sects are recognized as consisting completely of *conscientious objectors* to military service. Quakers and Mennonites are the most well-known of such sects. In adopting the 1940 Selective Training and Service Act Congress broadened the exemption restricted to conscientious objectors who were affiliated with "well-recognized religious sects or organizations" by making it unnecessary to belong to a pacifist religious sect if the claimant's own opposition to war was based on "religious training and belief." The Congress recognized that one might be religious without belonging to an organized church just as surely as minority members of a faith not opposed to war might through religious reading reach a conviction against participation in war. There has, however, been a problem about interpreting the phrase "religious training and belief" which Congress has defined as "belief in a relation to a Supreme Being involving duties superior to those arising from any human relation." The statute excludes those whose opposition to war stems from a "merely personal moral code."

Ecclesiastical courts have no legal authority, and exist only to pass on matters of internal concern to a religious group. So long as their procedures and judgments are in accord with their own established rules, the courts will not entertain actions to relieve from their decisions.

The Courts

In the absence of other public records, *church records* are accepted as attesting to birth, baptismal, death and other dates.

Under the common law no privilege is extended to clergymen to withhold *confidential communications or confessions*. However, all courts recognize the right of a clergyman to keep such communications secret, provided always that they were entrusted to him in his official capacity and according to the established discipline of his church. Many states have statutes so providing.

This same right has been extended to elders of the church who, although not ordained into the profession, are at times called upon to conduct some of the clerical functions of their church.

The New York statute, copied by some other states, expressly declares: "A clergyman, or other minister of any religion, shall not be allowed to disclose a confession made to him, in his professional character, in the course of discipline, enjoined by the rules or practice of the religious body to which he belongs."

It has further been held that even when such confessions are voluntary and not made under mandate of church law, they remain inviolable. Courts will extend the same privilege even when the confessor is not a regular member of the clergyman's denomination. A Minnesota decision in this connection stated that "It is important that the communications be made in such spirit and within the course of 'discipline,' and if it is sufficient whether such discipline enjoins the clergyman to receive the communication or whether it enjoins the other party, if a member of the church, to deliver the communication. Such practice makes the communication privileged, when accompanied by the essential characteristics, though made by a person not a member of the particular church or of any church. Man, regardless of his religious affiliation, whose conscience is shrunken and whose soul is puny, enters the clergyman's door in despair and gloom; there he finds consolation and hope. It is said that God through the clergy resuscitates. The clergyman practices the thought that the finest of altars is the soul of any unhappy man who is consoled and thanks God."

Although early American jurisprudence tended to disqualify *witnesses* without belief in God or in ultimate punishment, most of the states have by law or court decision made atheists competent witnesses. In the states lacking such laws no person without belief in a Supreme Being or in devine punishment may testify. But it is always possible for a trial judge still to decide on the competency of a witness.

A witness averse to swearing may affirm, and be accorded equal credence with one who has taken the regular oath.

No inquiry on the specific beliefs of a witness, for the purpose of discrediting him, may be instituted. That is, no effort may be made to sway judge or jury of a certain religious faith by intimations that the witness does not accept their theological notions, or belong to a church. Only where such matters have immediate and direct bearing on the witness's competence are they permissible.

Aspersions of the religion of a party are grounds for reversal. Calling a party "Christ-killer" or using similar epithets in a trial is an appeal to prejudice that calls for a reversal of judgment for a new trial.

Mere profession of a certain faith is not sufficient for acceptance or disqualification of a juror. It is improper to ask of a talesman whether he would more readily believe the testimony of a member of one sect than that of a witness of another sect.

However, inquiries on religion are permitted when they may guide an attorney to intelligent exercise of peremptory challenges relevant to issues in the case.

Though at common law last words of non-believers were not judicially accepted, American law has modified that attitude. If the deceased would have been able to testify competently on the matters at issue had he lived, his declaration becomes admissible.

Judge and jury may then pass upon the state of mind of the declarant before death, and on the credibility of his words.

When the purpose is to protect the community in its enjoyment of rest and quiet on the generally recognized day of rest it is a legitimate exercise of the police power of government in the interest of health, peace, general welfare of the community. There may be the objective of preventing disturbances of religious worship, but not of facilitating the imposition of a duty of religious worship; not unreasonably restricting activities necessary to the welfare of the community; nor fostering

19

economic discrimination. But many *Sunday laws* have by interpretation, as well as by their express terms, the effect of prohibiting certain enjoyments (such as concerts of non-religious music) rather than simply abstinence from work or business activity.

A number of states permit persons whose religions observe another rest day than Sunday, relief from the necessity of keeping the Sunday laws. In Indiana, Kansas, Kentucky, Massachusetts, Michigan, Missouri, Nebraska, New York, North Dakota, Ohio, Oklahoma, Rhode Island, Texas, Utah, Washington, West Virginia, and Wisconsin, those who fully observe another day may labor on Sunday-even common labor in Nebraska.

Obviously, the "other day" is the Jewish sabbath, also observed by certain Christian sects such as the Seventh Day Adventists and Baptists. Ohio, Texas, Virginia, West Virginia, and Wisconsin specify the "seventh day"; and Rhode Island and Virginia refer specifically to Jews.

All such exemptions are obviously limited by the need for avoiding disturbances of worship, or the creation of any other form of public annoyance.

The wording of most Sunday legislation, and many court judgments, indicate that compulsory Sunday rest, industrial, commercial, theatrical, and athletic, originated in efforts to uphold the religious character of Sunday, the social values being incidental and sometimes a late afterthought.

Time, however, has brought about many changes in *blue-law* attitudes, and there has been a letting-down of the bars involving many matters considered necessary activity and conducive to the general well-being (works of necessity or mercy). Most business activity is permitted in most states on Sundays. Liquor stores are the main if not the only commercial enterprise which do no business on Sunday.

The trend is to accord Jews, Seventh Day Adventists, and other groups observing another day than Sunday the right to keep their own Sabbaths. Both federal and state legislation protects workers who cannot work on Saturdays because of their faith from losing unemployment benefits if they leave their jobs because the employers insist that they work on those sabbath days or be terminated.

We are told by the word of the gospel
that in this His fold there are two swords,
a spiritual, namely, and a temporal. . .
the one, indeed, to be wielded . . .
by the hand of the priest, the other by
the hand of kinds and knights . . .

Pope Bonifact VIII, *Unam Sanctam* (1302)

Chapter 2

ASPECTS OF THE LAW OF RELIGIOUS "CULTS"

The recent revival of religious enthusiasm in the United States has spawned public and legal controversy about the practices of some religious sects. The totality of the commitment of the members of these groups have evoked accusations of "mind control" and "brainwashing" against cult leaders. Although the religious orders have created a strong public dispute and discord in many families, courts must consider the legal rights of the parties involved--in the sect as well as the parents and the youthful worshipper--and neither be influenced by the reluctance of society to accept the novel and unusual, nor swayed by parents lamenting the flight of their child.

Although the departure of a youth from a conventional lifestyle to a totalitarian, ascetic existence might suggest emotional conflict or social abberrance, the religious sect does not commit a crime by simply offering an alternative mode of living.

Sect practices usually entail extensive prayer, discussion, study, and meditation. A few of the religions demand such austerity and commitment that some parents and critics suspect the groups of unnatural, involuntary, and perhaps, illegal indoctrination techniques.

Most of these new personality alterations of the novices, the ← poor gram intensity of proselytization and indoctrination, the totality of commitment to the group, and the sometimes aggressive solicitation of funds and public distribution of literature. Parents of group adherents, sympathetic public officials, and some members of the mental health community contend that the indoctrinees are victims of illegal "brainwashing" and

22

hypnotic treatments administered by these religions. Sect members have also been charged with violating ordinances prohibiting unlicensed solicitation, distribution of literature, and public gatherings.

Whether the controversial practices of the new religions present substantive issues of criminal or civil liability depends upon the scope of legal protection afforded religious activity. While the free exercise clause of the First Amendment absolutely protects even irrational and occult religious beliefs and doctrine so that unconventional religions such as the Krishna movement are constitutionally protected, still a court could find certain religious practices to be criminal if they jeopardize the interest of the state in public health, safety, order or welfare. Beyond this, despite good faith pretentions of modern religious groups, their leaders, or their acolytes, religious practices that interfere with the personal or property rights of another person could form the basis for various actions for intentional torts.

But in addition to the potential criminal and civil liability of the religious groups, parents who resort to self-help by forcibly removing children from a sect could also incur liability. Parents frequently employ professional abductors, who call themselves "deprogrammers." In a number of situations the subjects of these "rescue" missions react with hostility, and several irate worshippers have lodged criminal complaints of kidnapping and false imprisonment against the deprogrammer and their collaberating parents.

Parents have also attempted to remove their offspring from religious societies by instituting various kinds of legal actions. For instance, parents of one religious devotee sought a writ of habeas corpus directing the Unification Church to present their daughter in court. The court dismissed the writ because the petitioners had failed to present evidence that the sect had exerted "control or restraint" over their daughter.

But despite accusations by opponents of the new religions, only a narrow range of activity could constitute the basis of a criminal action against a religious sect.

Applying various standards and criteria derived from the free exercise clause of the First Amendment, courts have nevertheless upheld statutory prohibitions of certain religious practices. For example, polygamy, although a doctrine of the Church of Jesus Christ of Latter-Day Saints, has been outlawed because courts have determined that the practice is immoral and detrimental to family solidarity in light of community values. Courts have also upheld the constitutionality of ordinances banning extreme tests of true religious faith, such as handling poisonous vipers, because such practices endanger public health and safety. The clause is held not to preclude the state from prohibiting religious practices that endanger participants as well as third parties. Thus the state enjoins the handling of snakes during religious services as a public nuisance. With the exception of the Native American Church (an American Indian sect), the use of drugs to stimulate or induce the transcendental experience has been held illegal. If a fringe sect, therefore, engaged in activities that are violent or perverse, the group could not seriously maintain the defense of permissible religious practice. In short, then, if a cult follows a religious practice that threatens the health of a member or that deviates so drastically from a community practice as to be repugnant to public welfare, the activity is suspect, and the cult or its individual members could incur criminal liability.

In any event, no court has ever imposed criminal liability upon a religious group because of its proselytization and indoctrination techniques. As long as the indoctrination is voluntary, the motivation of an individual for joining even an extreme religious group is not subject to judicial review. The First Amendment protects the parties. Furthermore, initiation procedures and conditions of membership are exclusively matters of ecclesiastical discipline. So while the sublime influence of a spiritual advisor upon an aged and infirm donor of property may affect the validity of the conveyance, the influence of a religious group on an indoctrinee cannot form the basis of criminal liability, because persuasion alone is beyond judicial scrutiny.

Courts have recognized actions for intentional torts (*civil liability*), however, where the religious activity of an individual or group infringes upon the civil rights of another member of ex-member. Equitable relief may be available to an ex-member.

24

One intentional tort for which a religious cult could be held liable is false imprisonment. False imprisonment is a wrong against the liberty of a person and so consists of an unlawful detention.

Whether or not the present vast array of religious cults will continue to exist in the coming years and even go on to exist for as long as the major religions have endured, their presence at the present time evokes volatile responses in our society. Their right to exist and even to expand is clear under the First Amendment. The questionable activities and practices are not protected for these cults as they are not for any religion. Those who seek to bring court challenges will have to produce evidence no different from the kind of evidence that has always been required to justify limiting or even eliminating the religious action of any religious sect.

Chapter 3

RELIGION AND PUBLIC EDUCATION

The question of the relationship of religion to the public schools has been before the courts from the very moment of the emergence of public education in the United States. The courts have responded to this always difficult and enduring question in a variety of ways and will probably continue to do so as an inevitable reflection of changing values in a pluralistic society such as ours. At best, then, what we can attempt here is to identify the most recent trends in judicial thinking and to isolate some of the legal principles upon which these trends are premised.

Bible Reading

In 1963, the United States Supreme Court came to grips for the first time with the substantive issue of Bible reading in the public schools. *School District of Abington v. Schempp*, 83 S. Ct. 1560, struck down Bible reading exercises in public schools and thereby invalidated practices as old as the public school system itself and also one of the most widespread religiously oriented programs common to many public schools. The *Schempp* decision profoundly affected state laws and educational programming in many states. The decision reflects a sophisticated awareness on the Court's part of the increasing pluralism of American society and the clear doctrinal differences among sects as to which is the "true" version of the Bible.

At the time of the *Schempp* ruling the constitutions and statutes of the states reflected an abiding desire to keep public funds from supporting sectarian institutions of any type. These enactments, however, were ambiguous as to what practices constituted sectarian instruction.

Thus, when the Court finally acted on the subject, thirty-seven states permitted Bible reading in their public schools. In only eleven states were Bible-reading exercises regarded as sectarian instruction prior to the *Schempp* decision. The high court of eight states found such exercises to violate either the states' constitutions or statutes. On the other hand, the courts of fourteen states upheld the constitutionality of Bible-reading exercises. The overwhelming number of states courts which had upheld programs of this nature before 1963, however, insisted that the reading be done without comment, and attendance could not be made compulsory.

The state courts upholding Bible-reading exercises shared a number of underlying premises. The major one was that the Bible was not a sectarian book since they could seen no significant differences between the King James version of the Protestants and the Douay version of the Catholics. Since Christianity was so interwoven in the fabric of our government, these courts concluded, to prohibit such practices would violate our historic traditions. Beyond this, the courts felt that Bible reading was important to an understanding of history and literature.

Prior to the *Schempp* decision, the state courts which struck down this practice as unconstitutional found the Bible clearly sectarian and concluded that such practices violated the religious sensibilities of non-Christians as well as nonbelievers. Programs of this nature violated the American tradition of church-state spearation because in practice the King James version of the Bible was the one normally used and it lacked the Apocryphal books of the Douay version as well as containing references to the Christology of the New Testament which is objectionable to the Jews. Moreover, the democracy of the classroom was destroyed even though such exercises were voluntary since self-exclusion stigmatized the non-participating student in the eyes of his peers for he was leaving because of apparent hostility to a book which was revered by those students remaining.

It is important to note that the United States Supreme Court in its decision in the *Schempp* case prohibit the use of the Bible in the study of history or literature. The Court said merely that the Bible could not be used as a *devotional* tool.

State courts which have ruled on this issue have all followed the *Schempp* doctrine and declared Bible-reading exercises in the public schools unconstitutional. This is one area of church-state relations affecting public education that is relatively settled.

Prayer

The most frequently asserted ground for upholding morning religious prayers in the classroom has been that it was not the intent of the constitutional framers to sever religion completely from government, but rather that the thing prohibited was state support of, or preference for, a particular religious denominational sect. So long as the exercises in question did not partake of the ceremonial practices of a particular religious or sectarian group, it was argued, they were not violative of constitutional guarantees of religious freedom.

In 1963, the United States Supreme Court ruled that a state sponsored prayer in the public school violated the establishment clause of the First Amendment. Speaking for the Court in the case of *Engle v. Vitale*, 370 U.S. 421, Mr. Justice Black noted that while the establishment clause and the free exercise clause might overlap in some instances, they forbid two quite different encroachments upon religious freedom. "The Establishment Clause," the Justice explained, "unlike the Free Exercise Clause, does not depend upon any showing of governmental compulsion and is violated by the enactment of laws which establish an official religion whether these laws operate directly to coerce nonobserving individuals or not. Inherent in this approach it would seem is the possibility the two clauses on religion might conflict with each other in a given situation, just as may the Freedom of Speech Clause and the Freedom of Religion Clause in other situations, for example."

Many of the critics of the Engel decision accused the Court of completely removing God from the classroom. But, again, the Court made it clear in its decision that nothing in its ruling should be construed as discouraging school children and others from reciting historical documents such as the Declaration of Independence, containing references to the Deity or singing "officially espoused anthems" which contain the composer's profession of faith in a Supreme Being.

Before this decision there had been a plethora of state court decisions on the subject dating from an 1884 decision of the Iowa Supreme Court in *Moore v. Moore*. Frequently such litigation in the states was meshed with the issue of whether Bible-reading exercises in the public schools violated the First Amendment. The only generalization that might safely be made concerning state court attitudes towards such programs is that the states in which such litigation arose were almost equally divided concerning their constitutional validity.

Despite the Supreme Court's ruling in the *Engel* case, the issue of prayer in the public schools cannot be regarded as settled from a practical viewpoint. For example, one Federal District Court ruled that prayer exercises which were voluntarily conducted either before or after the official school day, and which were not heralded by the official school bell, were not prohibited by the *Engel* ruling even though these programs were conducted in public school rooms. On the other hand, most recently in 1979 in New Jersey, a high school principal who allowed a group of students to conduct a prayer meeting in his office before the school day began was so prohibited both by the local Board of Education and supported by state county court.

Released Time

Some of the most common practices in the public school carrying religious overtones, especially since 1914 and until the United States Supreme Court's action in the *McCollum* and *Zorach* cases, have been those exercises known as released or dismissed time. Released time refers to programs whereby representatives of the various faiths, conducted on public school premises during the regular school day, for a period of time, instruction in the tenets of the particular sect. In most of such cases, student attendance in such programs was voluntary, and if a student did not attend he was required to remain in school (usually in the study-hall) and it was presumed he would study his secular subjects.

Dismissed time, on the other hand, consists of programs whereby public school students were dismissed from the school during regular school hours to attend programs of religious instruction off the premises of the public schools.

Mr. Justice Black, writing the majority opinion in *Illinois ex rel McCollum v. Board of Education*, 333 U.S. 203 (1948), held that a released time program such as described here constituted the "use of tax supported property for religious instruction and the close cooperation of the school authorities and the religious council in promoting religious instruction." Consequently, the Court held that the particular released time program at hand violated the establishment clause of the First Amendment and applicable to the states by the Due Process Clause of the Fourteenth Amendment.

Since the McCollum decision left small doubt that re-leased-time" programs are clearly unconstitutional, the next step seemed the adjudication of dismissed time. In 1952, in *Zorach v. Clauson*, 343 U.S. 306, the Supreme Court dealt with the whole issue of dismissed time for the first time. There, the New York Education Law provision which the New York City school board utilized to permit its public schools to release students during schools hours for religious instruction outside of the school building, and without the expenditure of public funds, was upheld against the contention that such a program violated the First Amendment made applicable to the states by the Fourteenth Amendment.

The court in finding that New York had neither prohibited the free exercise of religion nor made a law respecting an establishment of religion within the meaning of the First Amendment, declared that there was no evidence in this particular case that such a system involved the use of coercion to get such students to enroll in such religious instruction. "We are a religious people whose institutions presuppose a Supreme Being," declared Mr. Justice Douglas, speaking for a 6-to-3 majority, held that while the First Amendment prohibits governmental financing of religion or undertaking of religious instruction, it does not require governmental hostility to religion.

Public School Use of Church-Owned Buildings

The courts have generally held that the necessary use of a church or other sectarian building for public school purposes is not *per se* violative of laws guaranteeing religious freedom or enactments prohibiting public appropriations in aid of church or sectarian purposes. The courts are also in general agreement that the use of church property for public school purposes does no violence to laws prohibiting sectarian instruction in the public schools; nor does it constitute compulsory attendance upon a place of worship.

Authority to rent or lease property for public school purposes may be expressed or implied. When the statutes specify conditions under which a school board may rent or lease property they are held to be mandatory and exceptions will not be allowed. When the statutes are silent on the matter, it has generally been held that the grant of power by a legislature to a school board to maintain and operate public school implies authorization for school boards to rent or lease facilities, including church-owned buildings, at their discretion. However, it has been made patently clear that a public school conducted on property owned by a religious group must, in fact, remain under the jurisdiction and control of a board of education. It is clearly beyond the authority of a school board to abdicate its responsibility to maintain schools in favor of a church or sectarian group from which a building might be rented.

Religious Use of Public School Buildings

The use of school buildings and the possibilities of such use

31

violating the religion clause of the First Amendment is too complex and variegated to submit to meaningful generalizations. One must tend to view it on a case to case basis with careful attention paid to state statutory law as well as constitutions. This is especially true because the Supreme Court has remained aloof from the issues. This variance of judicial opinion is not surprising given the lack of uniformity of statutory coverage on the subject. It has been generally held by the courts that a legislative enactment allowing the use of school buildings for religious purposes, without interfering with the conduct of the educational enterprise, is not unconstitutional. In jurisdictions where the legislatures vest authority in boards of education to permit the use of public school buildings for religious purposes, it has been held that such enactments confer considerable discretionary power which, in the absence of abuse, is not subject to judicial review. Emphasized repeatedly by the courts has been the rule that a board of education may not in its discretion allow one religious group to use a schoolhouse and deny the use to other religious bodies.

In jurisdictions where the statutes have been silent on the subject of religious use of public school buildings, the courts are in disagreement as to the legality of such use. One line of authority holds that the utilization of public school buildings for purposes other than those connected with school operation is forbidden. On the other hand, some courts have decreed that such use is permissible.

In spite of the diversity of judicial reasoning on the subject, certain points of agreement are apparent in the decisions: (1) No one has an inherent right to the use of school buildings. Consequently, in the absence of enactments to the contrary, a board of education may properly disallow religious use of property under its jurisdiction. (2) If a board of education opens the doors of a schoolhouse for religious purposes, it must open them equally wide for all religious groups. Under the familiar doctrine that in the exercise of its discretionary power a board of education may not be arbitrary, unreasonable, or discriminatory, the courts are in agreement that similar privileges must be afforded to all within a class. (3) The use of a school building for religious purposes may not interfere with the conduct of a school.

Public School Teachers

On the ground of governmental neutrality in religious matters, the courts have almost consistently held that a teacher may not engage in sectarian religious instruction or disseminate sectarian literature in a public school classroom. Since freedom of action in religious matters is not so absolute as freedom of belief, the courts have not only enjoined religious propagandizing but have also held that a teacher will not be excused from the performance of contractual duties because such duties may be repugnant to his religious beliefs.

As to the permissibility of wearing a distinctive religious garb by public school teachers while engaged in the performance of duties, it is well established that a statute or administrative ruling prohibitive of such dress is not unconstitutional. In the absence of such regulations, however, the courts are divided on the issue. While some courts have held in the absence of a showing of sectarian instruction such garb is permissible, others have held that dress in itself constitutes an unlawful sectarian influence.

The courts have repeatedly stressed the fact that employment of teachers is a discretionary act of a board of education and, in the absence of a showing of bad faith, is not subject to judicial review. The power cannot be delegated, but must be exercised by a board as a corporate body.

Membership in a religious organization or in a religious order has not generally been held to disqualify a person from employment as a public school teacher. Also, that a teacher has professed vows of obedience to a religious superior does not constitute illegal sectarian control, and that the donation by a teacher of salary into the treasury of a religious organization does not constitute illegal expenditures of public funds, it has been generally agreed.

Related Religious School Activities

Some issues involving religion in the public schools have not reached the Supreme Court. Furthermore, the Court has not given a clear definition of what religion is. The Court has not ruled that all religious observances in the schools are unconstitutional; it has stated what schools cannot do, but it has not indicated what schools can do. The line separating the permissible from the forbidden has not been made clear.

1. *Study of Religious Literature.* Study about what people have done and what they have believed would be permissible. For example, describing what Martin Luther did in the early 1500's and showing cause-and-effect relationship with this crusade is necessary for an understanding of the Reformation. A discussion of the wisdom of his work would not be acceptable to some groups. Having books available for students to read is consistent with the Supreme Court ruling. It would be questionable whether or not a pupil could be required to read a religious classic which advocated a doctrine alien to his own.

2. *Religious Music.* This should not be played or sung as part of a devotional exercise. A school, however, could have recordings illustrative of the contributions that music has made to the arts and to civilization.

3. *Religious Pageants.* If presented in a religious way, such performances could not be upheld. It would seemingly be difficult to stage a sectarian play without infringing upon an individual's beliefs.

4. *Baccalaurate Services.* Many baccalaurate programs include a visiting minister who delivers the address and one or more preachers who assist in the service such by reading the scripture and praying. In addition, to the sermon, the scripture, and the prayer, sacred music is often sung. Some of the programs are held within the school while others are conducted in local churches. There is no question but that the exercises held within the school are in violation of the Supreme Court's decision in *Engel* and *Schempp*. To make attendance voluntary would still be an abridgment of the Court's holding. A school might continue to hold the service in a church and make

34

attendance voluntary. But the school, is involved in the program through planning and participation, so it is conceivable that the Court would overrule the exercise on the grounds that changing the locale of the program does not change the substance of it. Another position that might be taken is that the voluntary attendance and participation exerts, nonetheless, an indirect coercion to attend.

5. *Religious Holidays.* Two problems arise. One is the closing of school for a religious event; the other is releasing children from school to attend or to participate in the celebration during school time but away from school. Neither *Engel* and *Schempp* offers a suggestion about the legality of either. *Zorach* comes nearer to answering the second question. Justice Douglas held in that case that excusing students to attend religious classes during school time was a matter of cooperation between schools and the churches. The distinction in *Zorach* and in this situation is that the former involved religious curricular activities; the latter's concern is for an occasional absence from school for religious activities.

6. *Flag Salute.* Throughout world history the religious beliefs of some minorities have conflicted with demonstrations which the majority of the public have regarded as manifestations of patriotism. The United States is no exception, despite two specific provisions in its Bill of Rights designed to protect the rights of religious minorities. One such patriotic demonstration which has placed a particular strain upon certain religious sects in the United States has been the practice of holding compulsory flag-salute ceremonies.

The initiative for establishing an American flag-salute ceremony dates back to 1892, and New York passed the first "flag salute" statute in 1898. Support for ceremonies of this nature came generally from groups such as the American Legion, The Daughters of the American Revolution, and the Ku Klux Klan. Opposition to practices of this type came, on the other hand, from the teaching profession and some religious groups such as the Jehovah's Witnesses. In any event, by 1940, some ritual involving the flag was being used in the public schools of at least thirty states.

It was the Jehovah's Witnesses who generally sponsored the

litigation attacking state laws authorizing programs of compulsory flag saluting in the public schools arguing they violated the Freedom of Religion Clause of the First Amendment. They objected that this practice violated a tenent of their religious belief in that it constituted a form of idolatry. Their efforts met with universal failure in the state courts prior to the time the Supreme Court took the subject under examination. The state courts usually adopted the "secular regulation" standard which has as its essence the notion that ceremonies in public schools involving saluting the flag and the pledge of allegiance are patriotic rather than religious exercises.

The Supreme Court showed an early reluctance to enter the controversy. For example, the first case involving this issue reached the Court in 1937 but the Court dismissed it summarily in a *per curiam* opinion on the grounds that it did not pose a substantial federal question. In three later cases to come to the Supreme Court the Jehovah's Witnesses were equally unsuccessful since the Court either upheld the lower courts' decisions permitting such exercises or dismissed the appeals for want of a substantial federal question.

Not until 1940 did the Supreme Court rule on the merits of compulsory flag-salute programs in the public schools. In the *Minersville School District v. Gobitis* (310 U.S. 586) case, the Court ruled 8-1 upholding constitutionality of such programs as non-violative of the Freedom of Religion Clause of the First Amendment. Concluding that "national unity is the basis of our security," and "that we live by symbols," the Court placed a higher priority on manifestations of patriotism than upon the injured religious sensibilities of a minority. Justice Stone, in dissenting concluded that while voluntary expressions of loyalty might promote national unity it was quite another thing to compel certain children to violate their religious beliefs to participate in these programs and regard this as more important than the Freedom of Religion Clause of the Constitution.

While before the Gobitis decision state courts had regularly upheld flag-salute exercises, following it, three state courts directly repudiated the ruling, and four others ignored the principle of the case and ruled in favor of the religious scruples of the Jehovah's Witnesses. In only two states did the courts follow the majority ruling of the Gobitis case and one of these cannot be considered a major case in point.

Two years after the Gobitis decision, several justices in a completely unrelated case undertook to state formally that they had changed their minds about their affirmative vote in the Gobitis case. Unsurprisingly, one year later in 1943, the Court reversed the Gobitis decision in *West Virginia State Board of Education v. Barnette*, 319 U.S. 624. Speaking for the majority, Justice Jackson held that compulsory programs of flag-saluting in the public schools invaded the spiritual and intellectual spheres of the individual in violation of the First Amendment.

Parchiaid. In 1971, 1973, and 1975 the Supreme Court decided major cases involving public funds and religious schools. The key case was in 1971, when the Court first was asked to decide a "parociaid" question.

With only one dissent the Supreme Court of the United States in 1971 declared unconstitutional a "purchase of secular services" statute in Pennsylvania and a "salary supplement" statute in Rhode Island. These two forms of "parochiaid" were held to violate the establishment of religion clause of the First Amendment. The primnary basis of the decision was a criterion which had first been formulated in a 1970 case involving tax exemption of religious property (*Walz v. Tax Commissioner,* 397 U.S. 664). The criterion was that there must not be excessive entanglement between government and religion. To determine whether the government entanglement with religion is excessive it is necessary to examine the character and purposes of the institutions which are benefited, the nature of the aids that is provided, and the resulting relationship between the government and religious authority. The Court reviewed its prior holdings in the church-state-education area and concluded that they did not call for total separation. Here, however, it found that the parochial schools constituted an integral part of the religious mission of the Catholic Church and involved substantial religious activity and purpose. Schools of the Catholic Church were the sole beneficiaries in Rhode Island to the date of the case, and virtually so in Pennsylvania.

The Pennsylvania statute authorized the state superintendent of education to "purchase" specified "secular education services" from nonpublic schools. The state then directly reimbursed the nonpublic schools for their actual expenditures for teachers' salaries, textbooks, and instructional materials. The textbooks and materials, which were restricted to the areas of mathematics, modern foreign languages, physical science, and physical education, had to be approved by the state superintendent. In Rhode Island the state officials were authorized to supplement the salaries of teachers of secular subjects in nonpublic elementary schools by paying directly to the teacher an amount not in excess of fifteen per cent of his current annual salary. Recipients were required to be teachers in nonpublic schools at which the average per pupil expenditure on secular education was less than the average in the state's public schools. The salary could not exceed the maximum paid to teachers in the public schools and recipients were to be certified in substantially the same manner as public school teachers. Eligible teachers were required to teach only those subjects offered in the public schools and to use only materials which were used in the public schools.

The Court distinguished aid for teachers' salaries from "secular, neutral, or non-ideological services, facilities, or materials," Recalling that the majority of the Court had refused in a 1968 New York textbook case to make assumptions "on a meager record" about the religious content of textbooks the state might provide, the Court here said that teachers have a "substantially different ideological character than books." In terms of potential for involving some aspect of faith or morals in secular subjects a textbook's content is ascertainable but a teacher's handling of a subject is not. The Court took notice of the inherent conflict in functions when a teacher under religious control and discipline is faced with separating religious from secular aspects of pre-college education. Furthermore, the restrictions and surveillance necessary to ensure that that teachers play a non-ideological role give rise to the kind of entanglement which the Constitution does not permit. The Court observed that the history of government grants on a continuing basis indicates that such programs have almost always been accompanied by varying measures of control. Determining which expenditures of church-related schools are religious and which are secular creates an intimate and continuing relationship between church and state. Additionally, the Court discussed the divisive political potential of such programs. It observed that although political debate and division generally are normal and healthy manifestations of our way of government, protection against political division along religious lines was one of the principal purposes of the religion of the First Amendment.

The criterion of "excessive entanglement" has been the basis for invalidation of statutes in several states providing various forms of financial aid to parochial schools. "Its emergence as an independent test is significant in that its co-equal combination with the "primary effect" test *creates a constitutional Scylla and Charybdis which causes any state program designed to aid its parochial schools to find hazardous sailing." *Americans for Separation of Church and State v. Oakey*, 339 F. Supp. (545 (D. Vt. 1972).

Two months after the United States Supreme Court invalidated the Pennsylvania "purchase of secular services" statute the legislature enacted a "parent reimbursement" statute. The act provided for reimbursement of tuition payments to parents whose children attended a nonpublic school in the state if the school fulfilled state compulsory education requirements and did not discriminate on the ground of race, color, or national origin. Suit was brought by the same parent who had brought the successful challenge to the other statute. A three-judge federal district court held that the arrangement had a primary effect of advancing religion and therefore was unconstitutional. By a 6-3 vote the Supreme Court in 1973 affirmed. *Sloan v. Lemon*, 413 U.S. 825. Looking to the substance of the effects of the legislation rather than to its characterization by supporters, the Court stated that the state had singled out a class of its citizens for a special economic benefit. its basic intended consequence was to preserve and support religion-oriented institutions. The Court said it was plain that this was not like the sort of "indirect" and "incidental" benefits that flowed to sectarian schools from programs aiding *all* parents by supplying bus transportation and secular textbooks for their children. It noted that those benefits had been carefully restricted to the purely secular side of church-affiliated institutions and provided no special aid for those who had chosen to support religious schools.

Supreme Court decisions reflect a unanimous view that allowing public funds for schools which are clearly parochial in nature violates the state's constitution. But while the general judicial attitude of opposition to use of public funds for parochial schools is present when dealing with sectarian-supported colleges and universities, the decisions lack the decree of consistency that is present when parochial elementary and secondary schools are involved.

The majority of state courts have a much more permissive attitude toward the use of state funds for special schools of one sort or another, which are of a sectarian nature. It would appear that most state courts have adopted a double standard when applying the religious clauses of the state or national constitutions to orphans' homes, and schools for delinquent and neglected children, on the one hand, and general parochial elementary or secondary schools, on the other.

The Courts of three states have ruled that providing free water to parochial schools does not violate the religious provisions of the state constitutions. Another state court has permitted the use of public funds to support nurses' training programs in hospitals even though they are under the control of a religious sect. Still, another court upheld an authorization permitting a church to purchase future college buildings at a reduced price. On the other hand, however, the Oklahoma court prohibited the use of part of all students' tuition fees to help support the YMCA and the YWCA.

On the subject of tax exemption, given the opposition of some important religious denominations in recent years to exempting property owned by sects from real property taxes coupled with the more detailed analysis of the Supreme Court of the establishment clause of the First Amendment in recent years, it might be expected that the litigation potential area in this area may increase.

Summary

In addition to the basic holdings of the cases cited in this chapter, the Supreme Court has given some pertinent principles with respect to church-state relationships. To meet the test of constitutionality, legislative enactments providing for religion in education must have a secular purpose and primary effect that does not promote nor stifle religion. Any legislation providing, in the main, for a religious exercise, does not meet the test of constitutionality under the establishment clause.

The role of the state in a religious exercise in the public schools is a neutral one. The state does not favor one religion nor all religions over none. That is to say, in a classroom an unbeliever has equal standing with a believer. The school may not promote a religious belief or an exercise which favors or disfavors any sectarian group. It does not matter whether a school community is made up of a homogeneous religious population—what matters is state involvement.

Religious exercises providing for voluntary participation of pupils have no more constitutional standing than those without an excusal provision. Once the state promotes an activity, there is some degree of coercion for all to participate.

The Supreme Court has not stated that all religion shall be removed from the schools. It has not given precise limits as to what may or may not be done. The school must be committed to a principle of neutrality as it concerns religion; moreover, any study of religion must be objective. Beyond these guides, the Court opinions leave the matter to school officials who will decide, in more specific situations, whether or not activities will be held.

Appendix A

GUIDE TO DRAFTING ARTICLES OF
RELIGIOUS CORPORATIONS

Careful attention should be paid to the provisions of the constitution and to any nonprofit corporation act in the state of incorporation. A number os state prohibit by constitution the incorporation of a church or religious denomination and others expressly limit religious corporations to incorporation for the purpose of holding title to property.

In order that a religious corporation be recognized as a tax-exempt organization under Section 501, subdivision (c) (3) of the Internal Revenue Code, Section 508 thereof requires organizations seeking such status to file with the Secretary of the Treasury or his delegate. Failure to do so will result in treatment as a private foundation, the articles of which must expressly include a prohibition of the activities listed in Sections 4941-4945 of the Internal Revenue Code and must expressly require the corporation to distribute income in such a fashion so as not to incur a tax on undistributed income.

All tax-exempt organizations must file for an exemption ruling with the local district director of Internal Revenue in whose area is located the organization's principal office. Application should be made on Form 1023 and the accompanying instructions should be followed in detail. Two copies of each major document required to be furnished by the official application form should be attached to the application.

Checklist of Documents That Should Accompany Official Application for Determination of Exempt Status

1. Articles or certificate of incorporation.
2. Bylaws.
3. The latest financial statement showing asseys, receipts and disbursements of the organization.
4. Detailed statement of the activities or proposed activities of the organization.

5. Written declaration of the applications made under penalty of perjury.

Checklist of Matters to be Considered When Drafting Articles of Incorporation of A Religious Society

1. Name of proposed corporation.
2. Purpose or purposes for which corporation is organized.
3. Location of place where activities are to be conducted.
4. Number of trustees. - Method by which change in number of trustees may be made.
5. Names and post office addresses of trustees selected for the first year of the corporation's existence.
6. Name and post office address of resident agent on whom process against the corporation may be served.
7. Name and address of each incorporator.
8. Period of duration of corporation. - Perpetual.
9. Membership provisions. - Initial members.
   - Qualifications and classification. - Rights.
10. Financial pledge or obligation.
11. Qualifications, election, rights and duties of trustees and officers.. - Limitation of authority of trustees and officers. - Indemnification.
12. Appointment and authority of committees.
13. Meetings of trustees, officers, and members.
14. Manner of amending articles.
15. Charitable purposes, limitations, and powers in compliance with Internal Revenue Code Sections 501 subdivision (c) (3) and applicable tax regulations.
16. Disposition of assets on termination for exempt purposes.

Appendix B

SELECTED LEGAL FORMS FOR INCORPORATORS OF RELIGIOUS SOCIETIES

1. Minutes of Preliminary Meeting of Organizors

MINUTES OF PRELIMINARY MEETING OF ORGANIZERS
OF

_____/ *Proposed corporate name*

On _____, 19___, at _____o'clock, ____m., at _____/address/, City of _____, State of _____, a meeting of the organizers and proposed incorporators of the above-named religious corporation was held, at which the following persons were present: _____/ *list names and addresses/*. The meeting was held pursuant to a written notice signed by more than _____ members in good standing and read publicly to the members of the _____*(church, or as the case may be)* on _____ successive Sundays preceding this meeting, for the purpose of incorporation and election of _____ (trustees *or* directors) as a governing body of the corporation. _____/ *Name/* was elected chairman of the meeting: _____/ *Name/* was elected secretary of the meeting, and kept the minutes.

The chairman announced that the object of the meeting was to take the necessary preliminary steps to organize a nonprofit religious corporation under the laws of the State of _____, for the purpose of _____,/teaching the doctrine and philosophy of _____, maintaining religious worship in accordance in accordance with the traditions, customs, and beliefs of _____, and establishing and maintaining a _____ *(church, synagogue, temple, or as the case may be)* and school for divine worship and education of its members/.

The chairman then presented to the meeting a draft of

45

proposed _____ /articles or certificate/ of incorporation to be formed, and the draft was thereupon approved in substance and in form by all persons present, and was signed and duly acknowledged by the incorporators named therein, _____, _____, and _____, in the manner required by law. A copy of the _____/articles *or* certificate/ of incorporation so presented, approved, and signed is attached hereto, marked Exhibit "A".

On motion duly made, seconded, and unanimously carried, the secretary, being one of the incorporators, was directed to file the articles of incorporation in the office of _____/name of appropriate state office/, and also to _____/file *or* record/ a certified copy of the _____/articles *or* certificate/ after due certification by _____ /state official/, in _____ /designate each county office or other office where copy to be filed or recorded./

On motions duly made, seconded, and unanimously carried, the number of _____/trustees *or* directors/ of the proposed corporation was determined to be _____ The names, addresses, and duration of terms as _____/trustees *or* directors/ of the proposed corporation shall be as follows:

Name	Address	Term Expires
_____	_____	_____
_____	_____	_____
_____	_____	_____

It was unanimously agreed that additional meetings of the organizers would be held on call of the chairman, upon not less than _____/24 hours/ written notice to each organizer, at the same place.

There being no further business to come before the meeting, upon a motion the same was duly adjourned.

/Signatures of chairman and
secretary of meeting/

2. Articles of Incorporation - General Form

We, the undersigned natural persons of age _____/ *specify age required by applicable statute/* or more and _____/ *set forth residency requirements if any/* do hereby adopt the following articles of incorporation:

ARTICLE 1

The name of this religious corporation is _____.

ARTICLE 2

Name

The corporation is a nonprofit religious corporation.

ARTICLE 3

Authorization

This corporation shall proceed under _____ /*statutory citation/*, of the laws of the State of _____.

ARTICLE 4

Purpose

The purpose for which this corporation is organized shall be _____ /*statement of reasons for existence of religious society/*.

ARTICLE 5

Place of Worship

The post office address of the corporation's principal office and place of worship is _____ /*address*/. City of _____, State of _____.

ARTICLE 6

Nonstock of Corporation

This corporation shall be nonstock, and no dividends or pecuniary profits shall be declared or paid to the members thereof.

ARTICLE 7

Duration

The period of duration of this corporation is _____ /*perpetual or as the case may be*/.

ARTICLE 8

Trustees

The number of directors constituting the initial board of trustees of the corporation is _____, and the names and addresses of the persons who are to serve as the initial trustees are as follows:

Address	Address
_____	_____
_____	_____
_____	_____

ARTICLE 9

Election of Trustees

The manner in which the trustees are to be elected by the members is as follows: _____

ARTICLE 10

Corporate Officers

The general officers and their respective duties of the corporation shall be _____ /*discuss offices, terms of office, and duties of officers*/.

ARTICLE 11

Election of Officers

The officers shall be elected by the trustees, who shall first be elected by the members of the corporation.

ARTICLE 12

Membership Requirements

The method and conditions on which members shall be accepted, transferred, discharged, and removed shall be as follows: _____ /*discuss eligibility, qualifications, and duties of membership, voting and non-voting membership, active and inactive membership, withdrawal, transfer, and removal of membership privileges, and church covenants of membership, if any*/.

ARTICLE 13

Amendments

These articles may be amended in the manner provided by statute at the time of amendment.

ARTICLE 14

Incorporators

The names and addresses of the persons forming this corporation are as follows:

Name	Address
_____	_____
_____	_____
_____	_____

In witness whereof, we have affixed our seal and signed our names on _____, 19_____

/incorporators' signatures/

3. Constitution and Bylaws

Note: The governing body of a religious society may adopt a constitution and bylaws prescribing rules and regulations concerning the government of the society, its discipline, worship, and doctrine. Such constitution and bylaws are obligatory on members, congregations, and officers of the socieyt, and are given effect by the civil courts if reasonable and not inconsistent with or repugnant to the law.

CONSTITUTION OR BYLAWS OF RELIGIOUS SOCIETY

Article 1

Name

This religious organization shall be known as _____

Article 2

Purpose

The purpose of this _____ /*church, or other religious organization*/ shall be _____ /*statement of reason for existence of organization*/.

Article 3

Government

/*State government or religious organization, including any ecclesiastical body, membership in religious convention, and the role of the members of the society*/.

Article 4

Membership

/*State eligibility, qualifications, and duties of membership; voting and non-voting membership; active and inactive membership; covenants of membership; transfer, withdrawal, and removal of members*/.

Article 5

Denominational Affiliation

This organization shall be a member of the _____ /*religious denomination*/, _____

Article 6

Meetings

/State annual, quarterly, monthly, and special business meetings, method of giving notice thereof, quorum of eligible voters, percent required to pass on issues, rules of order, and also any weekly religious or devotional meetings/.

Article 7

Board of Trustees

/State composition, term of office, elections, duties, powers, and limitations/.

Article 8

Officers and staff

/State offices and staff positions; length of terms; powers and duties of officers; duties and responsibilities of staff; nomination, election removal, and resignation of officers/.

Article 9

Minister or Pastor or Rabbi

/State qualifications, manner of selection, tenure, duties, dismissal, and resignation/.

Article 10

Organization

/State various departments and committees, composition and duties of each, chairman's duties, and functions of each/.

Article 11

Disposition of Property

[State the disposition of real and personal property of the religious organization should it cease to be a member of the denomination, conference, or convention, or upon dissolution].

Appendix C
RELIGIOUS CLAUSES IN SELECTED
STATE CONSTITUTIONS

CONSTITUTION OF ALASKA
1959
PREAMBLE

We, the people of Alaska, grateful to God...in order to secure and transmit to succeeding generations our heritage of...religious liberty...

ARTICLE I. DECLARATION OF RIGHTS

Sec. 3. Civil rights. No person is to be denied the enjoyment of any civil or political right because of race, color, creed, or national origin. The legislature shall implement this section.

Sec. 4. Freedom of religion. No law shall be made respecting an establishment of religion, or prohibiting the free exercise thereof.

ARTICLE VII. HEALTH, EDUCATION, AND WELFARE

Sec. 1. Public education. The legislature shall by general law establish and maintain a system of public schools open to all children of the State, and may provide for other public educational institutions. Schools and institutions so established shall be free from sectarian control. No money shall be paid from funds for the direct benefit of any religious or other private educational institution.

ARTICLE IX. FINANCE AND TAXATION

Sec. 4. Exemptions...All, or any portion of, property used exclusively for non-profit religious, charitable, cemetery, or educational purposes as defined by law, shall be exempt from taxation. Other exemptions of like or different kind may be granted by general law. All valid existing exemptions shall be retained until otherwise provided by law.

Sec. 6. Public Purpose. No tax shall be levied, or appropriation of public money made, or public property transferred, nor shall the public credit be used, except for a public purpose.

CONSTITUTION OF ARIZONA
1912
PREAMBLE

We, the people of the State of Arizona, grateful to Almighty God for our liberties...

ARTICLE II. DECLARATION OF RIGHTS

Sec. 7. Oaths and affirmations. The mode of administering an oath, or affirmation, shall be such as shall be most consistent with and binding upon the conscience of the person to whom such oath, or affirmation, may be administered.

Sec. 12. Liberty of conscience; appropriations for religious purposes prohibited; religious freedom. The liberty of conscience secured by the provisions of this Constitution shall not be so construed as to excuse acts of licentiousness, or justify practices inconsistent with the peace and safety of the State. No public money or property shall be appropriated for or applied to any religious worship, exercise or instruction, or to the support of any religious establishment. No religious qualification shall be required for any public office or employment, nor shall any person be incompetent as a witness or juror in consequence of his opinion on matters of religion, nor be questioned touching his religious belief in any court of justice to affect the weight of his testimony.

ARTICLE IX. PUBLIC DEBT, REVENUE AND TAXATION

Sec. 2. There shall be exempt from taxation all federal, state, county and municipal property. Property of educational, charitable and religious associations or institutions not used or held for profit may be exempt from taxation by law...

Sec. 10. Aid of church, private or sectarian school, or public service corporation. No tax shall be laid or appropriation of public money made in aid of any church, or private or sectarian school, or any public service corporation.

ARTICLE XI. EDUCATION

Sec. 7. Sectarian instruction; religious or political test or qualification. No sectarian instruction shall be imparted in any school or State educational institution that may be established under this Constitution, and no religious or political test or qualification shall ever be required as a condition of admission into any public educational institution of the State, as teacher, student, or pupil; but the liberty of conscience hereby secured shall not be so construed as to justify practices or conduct inconsistent with the good order, peace, morality, or safety of the State, or with the rights of others.

ARTICLE XX. ORDINANCE

First. Toleration of religious sentiment. Perfect toleration of religious sentiment shall be secured to every inhabitant of this State, and no inhabitant of this State shall be molested in person or property on account of his or her mode of religious worship, or lack of the same.

Second. Polygamy. Polygamous or plural marriages, or polygamous cohabitation are forever prohibited within this State.

Seventh. Public school system; suffrage. Provisions shall be made by law for the establishment and maintenance of a system of public schools which shall be open to all the children of the State and be free from sectarian control, and said schools shall always be conducted in English. . . .

CONSTITUTION OF ARKANSAS
1874
PREAMBLE

We, the people of the State of Arkansas, grateful to Almighty God for the privilege of choosing our own form of government, for our civil and religious liberty...

ARTICLE II. DECLARATION OF RIGHTS

Sec. 24. Religious liberty. All men have a natural and indefeasible right to worship Almighty God according to the dictates of their own consciences; no man can, of right, be compelled to attend, erect or support any place of worship; or to maintain any ministry against his consent. No human authority can, in any case or manner whatsoever, control or interfere with the right of conscience; and no preference shall ever be given, by law, to any religious establishment, denomination or mode of worship above any other.

Sec. 25. Protection of religion. Religion, morality and knowledge being essential to good government, the General Assembly shall enact suitable laws to protect every religious denomination in the peaceable enjoyment of its own mode of public worship.

Sec. 26. Religious tests. No religious test shall ever be required of any person as a qualification to vote or hold office, nor shall any person be rendered incompetent to be a witness on account of his religious belief; but nothing herein shall be construed to dispense with oaths or affirmations.

ARTICLE XVI. FINANCE AND TAXATION

Sec. 5. Tax exemptions. ...Provided, further, that the following property shall be exempt from taxation; Public property used exclusively for public purposes; churches used as such; cemeteries used exclusively as such; school buildings and apparatus; libraries and grounds used exclusively for school purposes, and building and grounds and materials used exclusively for public charity.

ARTICLE XIX.   MISCELLANEOUS PROVISIONS

Sec. 1. Atheists disqualified from holding office or testifying as witness. No person who denies the being of a God shall hold any office in the civil departments of this State nor be competent to testify as a witness in any court.

CONSTITUTION OF CALIFORNIA
1879
PREAMBLE

We, the People of the State of California, grateful to Almighty God...

ARTICLE I.   DECLARATION OF RIGHTS

Sec. 4. Liberty of conscience. The free exercise and enjoyment of religious profession and worship, without discrimination or preference, shall forever be guaranteed in this State; and no person shall be rendered incompetent to be a witness or juror on account of his opinions on matters of religious belief; but the liberty of conscience hereby secured shall not be so construed as to excuse acts of licentiousness, or justify practices inconsistent with the peace or safety of this State.

ARTICLE IV.   LEGISLATIVE DEPARTMENT

Sec. 22. Appropriations...no state aid for private institutions; exceptions. ...no money shall ever be appropriated or drawn from the State Treasury for the purpose or benefit of any corporation, association, asylum, hospital, or any other institution not under the exclusive management and control of the State as a state institution, nor shall any grant or donation of property ever be made thereto by the State except that notwithstanding anything contained in this or any other section of the Constitution

(1) Federal-state funds for hospital construction...
(2) Aid to institutions for support and maintenance of orphans, half-orphans, abandoned children, and children of needy parents. . . .
(3) Aid to needy blind persons. . . .
(4) Aid to needy physically handicapped persons. . . .
(5) State's right to inquire into management of institutions. . . .

Sec. 30. Public aid for sectarian purposes prohibited. Neither the Legislature, nor any county, city and county, township, school district, or other municipal corporation, shall ever make any appropriation, or pay from any public fund whatever, or grant anything to or in aid of any religious sect, church, creed, or sectarian purpose, or help to support or sustain any school, college, university, hospital, or other institution controlled by any religious creed, church, or sectarian denomination whatever; nor shall any grant or donation of personal property or real estate ever be made by the State, or any city, city and county, town, or other municipal corporation for any religious creed, church, or sectarian purpose whatever; provided that nothing in this section shall prevent the Legislature granting aid pursuant to Section 22 of this article.

ARTICLE IX. EDUCATION

Sec. 8. No public money for sectarian schools. No public money shall ever be appropriated for the support of any sectarian or denominational school, or any school not under the exclusive control of the officers of the public schools; nor shall any sectarian or denominational doctrine be taught, or instruction thereon be permitted, directly or indirectly, in any of the common schools of this State.

Sec. 9. University of California. . . . The university shall be entirely independent of all political or sectarian influence and kept free therefrom in the appointment of its regents and in the administration of its affairs. . . .

ARTICLE XIII. REVENUE AND TAXATION

Sec. 1½. Exemption of church property; church buildings under construction; parking lots. All buildings and equipment, and so much of the real property on which they are situated as may be required for the convenient use and occupation of said buildings, when the same are used solely and exclusively for religious worship, and any building and its equipment in the course of erection, together with the land on which it is located as may be required for the convenient use and occupation of the building, if such building, equipment and land are intended to be used solely and exclusively for religious worship, and, until the Legislature shall otherwise provide by law, that real property owned by the owner of the building which the owner is required by law to make available for, and which is necessarily and reasonably required and exclusively used for the parking of the automobiles of persons while attending or engaged in religious worship in said building whether or not said real property is contiguous to land on which said building is located, and which real property has not been rented or used for any commercial purpose at any other time during the preceding year, shall be free from taxation; provided that no building so used or, in the course of erection, intended to be so used, its equipment or the land on which it is located, which may be rented for religious purposes and rent received by the owner therefor, shall be exempt from taxation.

CONSTITUTION OF COLORADO
1876
PREAMBLE

We the people of Colorado with profound reverence for the Supreme Ruler of the Universe...

ARTICLE II. BILL OF RIGHTS

Sec. 4. Religious freedom. The free exercise and enjoyment of religious profession and worship, without discrimination, shall forever hereafter be guaranteed; and no person shall be denied any civil or political right, privilege or capacity, on account of his opinions concerning religion; but the liberty of conscience hereby secured shall not be construed to dispense with oaths or affirmations, excuse acts of licentiousness or justify practices inconsistent with the good order, peace or safety of the state. No person shall be required to attend or support any ministry or place of worship, religious sect or denomination against his consent. Nor shall any preference be given by law to any religious denomination or mode of worship.

ARTICLE V. LEGISLATIVE DEPARTMENT

Sec. 34. Appropriations to Private Institutions Forbidden. No appropriation shall be made for charitable, industrial, educational or benevolent purposes to any person, corporation or community not under the absolute control of the state, nor to any denominational or sectarian institution or association.

ARTICLE IX. EDUCATION

Sec. 7. Aid to private schools, churches, sectarian purposes, forbidden. Neither the general assembly, nor any county, city, town, township, school district or other public corporation, shall ever make any appropriation, or pay from any public fund or moneys whatever, anything in aid of any church or sectarian society, or for any sectarian purpose, or to help support or sustain any school, academy, seminary, college, university or other literary or scientific institution, controlled by any church or sectarian denomination whatsoever; nor shall any grant or donation of land, money or other personal property, ever be made by the state, or any such public corporation to any church, or for any sectarian purpose.

Sec. 8. Religious test and race discrimination forbidden; sectarian tenets. No religious test or qualification shall ever be required of any person as a condition of admission into any public education institution of the state, either as a teacher or student; and no teacher or student of any such institution shall ever be required to attend or participate in any religious service whatever. No sectarian tenets or doctrines shall ever be taught in the public schools, nor shall any distinction or classification of pupils be made on account of race or color.

ARTICLE X. REVENUE

Sec. 5. Property used for religious worship, schools and charitable purposes exempt. Property real and personal, that is used solely and exclusively for religious worship, for schools or for strictly charitable purposes, also cemeteries not used or held for private or corporate profit, shall be exempt from taxation, unless otherwise provided by general law.

ARTICLE XVII. MILITIA

Sec. 5. Exemptions in time of peace. No person having conscientious scruples against bearing arms, shall be compelled to do militia duty in time of peace; provided, such person shall pay an equivalent for such exemption.

CONSTITUTION OF CONNECTICUT
1818
PREAMBLE

The people of Connecticut acknowledging with gratitude, the good providence of God, in having permitted them to enjoy a free government...

ARTICLE FIRST. DECLARATION OF RIGHTS

Sec. 3. Religious liberty. The exercise and enjoyment of religious profession and worship, without discrimination, shall forever be free to all persons in this state; provided, that the right hereby declared and established, shall not be so construed as to excuse acts of licentiousness, or to justify practices inconsistent with the peace and safety of the state.

Sec. 4. No preferences in Christian sects or modes of worship. No preference shall be given by law to any Christian sect or mode of worship.

ARTICLE SEVENTH. OF RELIGION

Sec. 1. Compulsory support of religion prohibited; all denominations of Christians to have equal rights. It being the duty of all men to worship the Supreme Being, the Great Creator and Preserver of the Universe, and their right to render that worship, in the mode most consistent with the dictates of their consciences; no person shall by law be compelled to join or support, nor be classed with, or associated to, any congregation, church or religious association. But every person now belonging to such congregation, church, or religious association shall remain a member thereof until he shall have separated himself therefrom, in the manner hereinafter provided. And each and every society or denomination of Christians in this state, shall have and enjoy the same and equal powers, rights and privileges; and shall have power and authority to support and maintain the ministers or teachers

60

of their respective denominations, and to build and repair houses for public worship, by a tax on the members of any such society only, to be laid by a major vote of the legal voters assembled at any society meeting, warned and held according to law, or in any other manner.

Sec. 2. Right to separate from Christian societies or denominations. If any person shall choose to separate himself from the society or denomination of Christians to which he may belong, and shall leave a written notice thereof with the clerk of such society, he shall thereupon be no longer liable for any future expenses which may be incurred by said society.

ARTICLE EIGHTH. OF EDUCATION

Sec. 2. The school fund shall remain a perpetual fund. The fund, called the SCHOOL FUND, shall remain a perpetual fund, the interest of which shall be inviolably appropriated to the support and encouragement of the public, or common schools throughout the state, and for the equal benefit of all the people thereof...and no law shall ever be made, authorizing said fund to be diverted to any other use than the encouragement and support of public, or common schools, among the several school societies, as justice and equity shall require.

CONSTITUTION OF DELAWARE
1897
PREAMBLE

Through Divine goodness, all men have by nature the rights of worshipping and serving their Creator according to the dictates of their consciences...

ARTICLE I. BILL OF RIGHTS

Sec. 1. Freedom of religion. Although it is the duty of all men frequently to assemble together for the public worship of Almighty God; and piety and morality, on which the prosperity of communities depend are hereby promoted; yet no man shall or ought to be compelled to attend any religious worship, to contribute to the erection or support of any place of worship, or to the maintenance of any ministry, against his own free will and consent; and no power shall or ought to be vested in or assumed by any magistrate that shall in any case interfere with, or in any manner control the rights of conscience, in the free exercise of religious worship, nor a preference given by law to any religious societies, denominations, or modes of worship.

Sec. 2. Religious test for office not required. No religious test shall be required as a qualification to any office, or public trust, under this State.

ARTICLE VIII. REVENUE AND TAXATION

Sec. 1. ...Exemption for public welfare purposes...the General Assembly may by general laws exempt from taxation such property as in the opinion of the General Assembly will best promote the public welfare.

ARTICLE IX. CORPORATIONS

Sec. 4. Rights, privileges, immunities and estates. The rights, privileges, immunities and estates of religious societies and corporate bodies, except as herein otherwise provided, shall remain as if the Constitution of this State had not been altered.

ARTICLE X. EDUCATION

Sec. 3. Use of educational funds by religious schools; exemption of school property from taxation. No portion of any fund now existing, or which may hereafter be appropriated, or raised by tax, for educational purposes, shall be appropriated to, or used by, or in aid of any sectarian, church or denominational school; provided, that all real or personal property used for school purposes, where the tuition is free, shall be exempt from taxation and assessment for public purposes.

Sec. 4. Use of public school fund. No part of the principal or income of the Public School Fund, now or hereafter existing, shall be used for any other purpose than the support of free public schools.

CONSTITUTION OF FLORIDA
1887
PREAMBLE

We, the people of the State of Florida, grateful to Almighty God...

DECLARATION OF RIGHTS

Sec. 5. Religious freedom; liberty of conscience, etc. The free exercise and enjoyment of religious profession and worship shall forever be allowed in this State, and no person shall be rendered incompetent as a witness on account of his religious opinions; but the liberty of conscience hereby secured shall not be so construed as to justify licentiousness or practices subversive of, or inconsistent with, the peace or moral safety of the State or society.

Sec. 6. Religious preferences; public aid, etc. No preference shall be given by law to any church, sect or mode of worship and no money shall ever be taken from the public treasury directly or indirectly in aid of any church, sect or religious denomination or in aid of any sectarian institution.

ARTICLE IX. TAXATION AND FINANCE

Sec. 1. Uniform and equal rate of taxation; special rates. The Legislature shall provide for a uniform and equal rate of taxation...and shall prescribe such regulations as shall secure a just valuation of all property, both real and personal, excepting such property as may be exempted by law for municipal, educational, literary, scientific, religious or charitable purposes.

CONSTITUTION OF ILLINOIS
1870
PREAMBLE

We, the people of the State of Illinois—grateful to Almighty God for the civil, political and religious liberty which He hath so long permitted us to enjoy, and looking to Him for a blessing upon our endeavors to secure and transmit the same unimpaired to succeeding generations, . . .

ARTICLE II. BILL OF RIGHTS

Sec. 3. Religious freedom. The free exercise and enjoyment of religious profession and worship, without discrimination, shall forever be guaranteed; and no person shall be denied any civil or political right, privilege or capacity, on account of his religious opinions; but the liberty of conscience hereby secured shall not be construed to dispense with oaths or affirmations, excuse acts of licentiousness, or justify practices inconsistent with the peace or safety of the State. No person shall be required to attend or support any ministry or place of worship against his consent nor shall any preference be given by law to any religious denomination or mode of worship.

ARTICLE VII. EDUCATION

Sec. 3. Public funds for sectarian purposes forbidden. Neither the General Assembly nor any county, city, town, township, school district, or other public corporation, shall ever make any appropriation or pay from any public fund whatever, anything in aid of any church or sectarian purpose, or to help support or sustain any school, academy, seminary, college, university, or other literary or scientific institution, controlled by any church or sectarian denomination whatever; nor shall any grant or donation of land, money, or other personal property ever be made by the State, or any such public corporation, to any church, or for any sectarian purpose.

ARTICLE IX. REVENUE

Sec. 3. Tax exemptions. The property of the State, counties, and other municipal corporations, both real and personal, and such other property, as may be used exclusively for agricultural and horticultural societies, for school, religious, cemetery and charitable purposes, may be exempted from taxation; but such exemption shall be only by general law. . . .

ARTICLE XII. MILITIA

Sec. 6. Conscientious objectors. No person having conscientious scruples against bearing arms, shall be compelled to do militia duty in time of peace: Provided, such person shall pay an equivalent for such exemption.

CONSTITUTION OF INDIANA
1851
PREAMBLE

We, the People of the State of Indiana, grateful to Almighty God . . .

ARTICLE I. BILL OF RIGHTS

right to worship Almighty God, according to the dictates of their own
Sec. 2. Right to worship. All men shall be secured in the natural consciences.

Sec. 3. Freedom of religion. No law shall, in any case whatever, control the free exercise and enjoyment of religious opinions, or interfere with the rights of conscience.

Sec. 4. Creedal preference. No preference shall be given, by law, to any creed, religious society, or mode of worship; and no man shall be compelled to attend, erect, or support, any place of worship, or to maintain any ministry, against his consent.

Sec. 5. Religious test for office. No religious test shall be required, as a qualification for any office of trust or profit.

Sec. 6. No state aid for religious institutions. No money shall be drawn from the treasury, for the benefit of any religious or theological institution.

Sec. 7. Religion no bar to competency of witnesses. No person shall be rendered incompetent as a witness, in consequence of his opinions on matters of religion.

ARTICLE 10. FINANCE

Sec. 1. Assessment and taxation. The General Assembly shall provide, by law, for a uniform and equal rate of assessment and taxation; and shall prescribe such regulations as shall secure a just valuation for taxation of all property, both real and personal, excepting such only for municipal, educational, literary, scientific, religious or charitable purpose, as may be specifically exempted by law.

ARTICLE 12. MILITIA

Sec. 6. Conscientious objectors. No person, conscientiously opposed to bearing arms, shall be compelled to do militia duty; but such person shall pay an equivalent for exemption; the amount to be prescribed by law.

We, the People of the State of Iowa, grateful to the Supreme Being for the blessings hitherto enjoyed, and feeling our dependence on Him for a continuation of those blessings, . . .

ARTICLE I. BILL OF RIGHTS

Sec. 3. Religion. The General Assembly shall make no law respecting an establishment of religion, or prohibiting the free exercise thereof; nor shall any person be compelled to attend any place of worship, pay tithes, taxes or other rates for building or repairing places of worship, or the maintenance of any minister, or ministry.

Sec. 4. Religious test; witnesses. No religious test shall be required as a qualification for any office, or public trust, and no person shall be deprived of any of his rights, privileges, or capacities, or disqualified from the performance of any of his public or private duties, or rendered incompetent to give evidence in any court of law or equity, in consequence of his opinions on the subject of religion; and any party to any judicial proceeding shall have the right to use as a witness, or take the testimony of, any other person not disqualified on account of interest, who may be cognizant of any fact material to the case; and parties to suits may be witnesses as provided by law.

ARTICLE VI. MILITIA

Sec. 2. Exemption. No person or persons conscientiously scrupulous of bearing arms shall be compelled to do military duty in time of peace; Provided that such person or persons shall pay an equivalent for such exemption in the same manner as other citizens.

CONSTITUTION OF KANSAS
1861
PREAMBLE

We, the people of Kansas, grateful to Almighty God . . .

BILL OF RIGHTS

Sec. 7. Religious liberty. The right to worship God according to the dictates of conscience shall never be infringed; nor shall any person be compelled to attend or support any form of worship; nor shall any control of or interference with the rights of conscience be permitted; nor any preference be given by law to any religious establishment or mode of worship. No religious test or property qualification shall be required for any office of public trust, nor for any vote at any election, nor shall any person be incompetent to testify on account of religious belief.

ARTICLE 6. EDUCATION

Sec. 8. Nonsectarianism. No religious sect or sects shall ever control any part of the common-school or university funds of the state.

ARTICLE 8. MILITIA

Sec. 1. Composition; exemption. The militia shall be composed of all able-bodied male citizens between the ages of twenty-one and forty-five years, except such as are exempted by the laws of the United States or of this state; but all citizens of any religious denomination whatever who from scruples of conscience may be averse to bearing arms shall be exempted therefrom, upon such conditions as may be prescribed by law.

ARTICLE 11. FINANCE AND TAXATION

Sec. 1. Exemption. All property used exclusively for state, county, municipal, literary, educational, scientific, religious, benevolent and charitable purposes, . . . shall be exempted from taxation.

ARTICLE 12. CORPORATIONS

Sec. 2. Liability of stockholders. Dues from corporations shall be secured by the individual liability of the stockholders to the amount of stock owned by each stockholder, and such other means as shall be provided by law; but such individual liability shall not apply to railroad corporations nor corporations for religious or charitable purposes.

Sec. 3. Religious corporations. The title to all property of religious corporations, shall vest in trustees, whose election shall be by the members of such corporations.

CONSTITUTION OF LOUISIANA
1921
PREAMBLE

We, the people of the State of Louisiana, grateful to Almighty God; . . .

ARTICLE 1. BILL OF RIGHTS

Sec. 4. Freedom of religion. Every person has the natural right to worship God according to the dictates of his own conscience. No law shall be passed respecting an establishment of religion, nor prohibiting the free exercise thereof; nor shall any preference ever be given to, nor any discrimination made against, any church, sect or creed of religion, or any form of religious faith or worship.

ARTICLE IV. LIMITATIONS

Sec. 8. Public funds; prohibited expenditure for sectarian, private, charitable or benevolent purposes; state charities; religious discrimination. No money shall ever be taken from the public treasury, directly or indirectly, in aid of any church, sect or denomination or religion, or in aid of any priest, preacher, minister or teacher thereof, as such, and no preference shall ever be given to, nor any discrimination made against any church, sect or creed of religion, or any form of religious faith or worship. No appropriation from the State treasury shall be made for private, charitable or benevolent purposes to any person or community; provided, this shall not apply to the State Asylums for the Insane, and the State Schools for the Deaf and Dumb and the Blind, and the Charity Hospitals, and public charitable institutions conducted under State authority.

Sec. 16. Forced heirship; abolition prohibited; adopted children; fidei commissa or trust estates; restrictions. . . . and provided that this prohibition as to trust estates or fidei commissas shall not apply to donations strictly for educational, charitable, religious purposes or trusts created by employers for the benefit of their employees . . .

ARTICLE X. REVENUE AND TAXATION

Sec. 4. Tax exemptions. The following property, and no other, shall be exempt from taxation.

1. Public property. All public property.

2. Religious, charitable and educational property. Places of religious worship, rectories and parsonages belonging to religious denominations and used as places of residence for ministers; places of burial; places devoted to charitable undertakings, including that of such organizations as lodges and clubs, schools, and colleges; but the exemption shall extend only to property, and grounds thereunto appurtenant, used for the above mentioned purposes, and not leased for profit or income. . . .

Sec. 8. License taxes; restrictions. License taxes may be levied on such classes of persons, association of persons and corporations pursuing any trade, business, occupation, vocation or profession, as the Legislature may deem proper, except . . . ministers of religion, . . .

ARTICLE XII. PUBLIC EDUCATION

Sec. 13. Public funds for private or sectarian schools; cooperative regional education. No public funds shall be used for the support of any private or sectarian school. Provided, that the Legislature may enact appropriate legislation to permit institutions of higher learning which receive all or part of their support from the State of Louisiana to engage in interstate and intrastate education agreements with other state governments, agencies of other state governments, institutions of higher learning of other state governments and private institutions of higher learning within or outside state boundaries.

ARTICLE XIV. PAROCHIAL AND MUNICIPAL AFFAIRS

Sec. 15. Civil service system; state; cities.

(A) (1) Appointments and promotions; examinations; discrimination. . . . no person in the State or City Classified Service shall be discriminated against or subjected to any disciplinary action for political or religious reasons, and all such persons shall have the right of appeal from such actions. . . .

CONSTITUTION OF MAINE
1820
PREAMBLE

Objects of government. We the people of Maine, . . . acknowledging with grateful hearts the goodness of the Sovereign Ruler of the Universe in affording us an opportunity, so favorable to the design; and imploring His aid and direction in its accomplishment, . . .

ARTICLE I. DECLARATION OF RIGHTS

Sec. 3. Religious freedom; proviso; sects equal; religious tests prohibited; religious teachers. All men have a natural and unalienable right to worship Almighty God according to the dicates of their own consciences, and no one shall be hurt, molested or restrained in his person, liberty or estate for worshipping God in the manner and season most agreeable to the dictates of his own conscience, nor for his religious professions or sentiments, provided he does not disturb the public peace, nor obstruct others in their religious worship;—and all persons demeaning themselves peaceably, as good members of the state, shall be equally under the protection of the laws, and no subordination nor preference of any one sect or denomination to another shall ever be established by law, nor shall any religious test be required as a qualification for any office or trust, under this state; and all religious societies in this state, whether incorporate or unincorporate, shall at all times have the exclusive right of electing their public teachers, and contracting with them for their support and maintenance.

ARTICLE VII. MILITARY

Sec. 5. Persons exempt from military duty. Persons of the denominations of Quakersand Shakers, justices of the supreme judicial court, ministers of the gospel and persons exempted by the laws of the United States may be exempted from military duty, but no other able-bodied person of the age of eighteen and under the age of forty-five years, excepting officers of the militia who have been honorably discharged shall be/so exempted unless he shall pay an equivalent to be fixed by law.

ARTICLE IX. GENERAL PROVISIONS

Sec. 1. Oaths and subscriptions; proviso; before whom to be taken. Every person elected or appointed to either of the places or offices provided in this constitution, and every person elected, appointed, or commissioned to any judicial, executive, military or other office under this state, shall before he enter on the discharge of the duties of his place or office, take and subscribe the following oath or affirmation: "I.............................. do swear, that I will support the Constitution of the United States and of this State, so long as I shall continue a citizen thereof. So help me God."

"I.......................... do swear, that I will faithfully discharge, to the best of my abilities, the duties incumbent on me as .... according to the Constitution and laws of the State. So help me God." Provided, that an affirmation in the above forms may be substituted, when the person shall be conscientiously scrupulous of taking and subscribing an oath. . . .

CONSTITUTION OF MARYLAND
1867
DECLARATION OF RIGHTS

We, the People of the State of Maryland, grateful to Almighty God for our civil and religious liberty, . . .

ARTICLE 36. Religious freedom. That as it is the duty of every man to worship God in such manner as he thinks most acceptable to Him, all persons are equally entitled to protection in their religious liberty; wherefore, no person ought by any law to be molested in his person or estate, on account of his religious persuasion, or profession, or for his religious practice, unless, under the color of religion, he shall disturb the good order, peace or safety of the State, or shall infringe the laws of morality, or injure others in their natural, civil or religious rights; nor ought any person to be compelled to frequent, or maintain, or contribute, unless on contract to maintain, any place of worship, or any ministry; nor shall any person otherwise competent, be deemed incompetent as a witness, or juror, on account of his religious belief; provided, he believes in the existence of God, and that under His dispensation such person will be held morally accountable for his acts, and be rewarded or punished therefor either in this world or in the world to come.

ARTICLE 37. Religious test as qualification for office; oath of office. That no religious test ought ever to be required as a qualification for any office of profit or trust in this State, other than a declaration of belief in the existence of God; nor shall the Legislature prescribe any other oath of office than the oath prescribed by this Constitution.

ARTICLE 38. Gifts, etc., for religious purposes. That every gift, sale or devise of land to any Minister, Public Teacher, or Preacher of the Gospel as such, or to any Religious Sect, Order or Denomination, or to, or for the support, use or benefit of, or in trust for, any Minister, Public Teacher, or Preacher of the Gospel, as such, or any Religious Sect, Order or Denomination; and every gift or sale of goods, or chattels to go in succession, or to take place after the death of the Seller or Donor, to or for such support, use or benefit; and also every devise of goods or chattels to or for the support, use or benefit of any Minister,

Public Teacher, or Preacher of the Gospel, as such, or any Religious Sect, Order or Denomination, without the prior or subsequent sanction of the Legislature, shall be void; except always, any sale, gift, lease or devise of any quantity of land, not exceeding five acres, for a church, meeting-house, or other house of worship, or parsonage, or for a burying ground, which shall be improved, enjoyed or used only for such purpose; or such sale, gift, lease or devise shall be void. Provided, however, that except in so far as the General Assembly shall hereafter by law otherwise enact, the consent of the Legislature shall not be required to any gift, grant, deed, or conveyance executed after the 2nd day of November, 1948, or to any devise or bequest contained in the will of any person dying after said 2nd day of November, 1948, for any of the purposes hereinabove in this Article mentioned.

ARTICLE 39. Manner of administering oath or affirmation. That the manner of administering an oath or affirmation to any person, ought to be such as those of the religious persuasion, profession, or denomination, of which he is a member, generally esteem the most effectual confirmation by the attestation of the Divine Being.

ARTICLE III.   LEGISLATIVE DEPARTMENT

Sec. 11. Ministers and persons holding civil offices under state not eligible as senators or delegates. No Minister of the Gospel, or of any religious creed, or denomination, and no person holding any civil office of profit, or trust, under this State, except Justices of the Peace, shall be eligible as Senator, or Delegate.

CONSTITUTION OF MASSACHUSETTS
1780
PREAMBLE

. . . .WE, therefore, the people of Massachusetts, acknowledging, with grateful hearts, the goodness of the Great Legislator of the Universe, in affording us, in the course of his Providence, . . .

PART THE FIRST.   A DECLARATION OF THE RIGHTS OF THE INHABITANTS OF THE COMMONWEALTH OF MASSACHUSETTS

ARTICLE II. Right and duty of public religious worship; protection therein. It is the right as well as the Duty of all men in society, publicly, and at stated seasons to worship the Supreme Being, the great Creator and preserver of the Universe. And no Subject shall be hurt, molested, or restrained, in his person, Liberty, or Estate, for worshipping God in the manner and season most agreeable to the Dictates of his own conscience, or for his religious profession or sentiments; provided he doth not Disturb the public peace, or obstruct others in their religious Worship.

ARTICLE III. Legislature empowererd to compel provision for public worship. As the happiness of a people, and the good order and preservation of civil government, essentially depend upon piety, religion and morality; and as these cannot be generally diffused through a Community, but by the institution of the public Worship of God, and of public instructions in piety, religion and morality: Therefore, to promote their happiness and to secure the good order and preservation of their government, the people of this Commonwealth have a right to invest their legislature with power to authorize and require, and the Legislature shall, from time to time, authorize and require the several Towns, Parishes, precincts, and other bodies politic, or religious societies, to make suitable provision, at their own Expense, for the institution of the Public worship of God, and for the support and maintenance of public protestant teachers of piety, religion and morality, in all cases where such provision shall not be made Voluntarily.—And the people of this Commonwealth have also a right to, and do, invest their legislature with authority to enjoin upon all the Subjects an attendance upon the instructions of the public teachers aforesaid, at stated times and seasons, if there be any on whose instructions they can Conscientiously and conveniently attend—Provided notwithstanding, that the several towns, parishes, precincts, and other bodies politic, or religious societies, shall, at all times, have the exclusive right of electing their public Teachers, and of contracting with them for their support and maintenance.—And all monies, paid by the Subject to the Support of public worship, and of the public teachers aforesaid shall, if he require it, be uniformly applied to the support of the public teachers of his religious sect or denomination, provided there be any on whose instructions he attends; otherwise it may be paid towards the support of the teacher or teachers of the parish or precinct in which the said monies are raised—And every denomination of Christians, demeaning themselves peaceably, and as good Subjects of the Commonwealth, shall be equally under the protection of the Law: And no subordination of any one sect or denomination to another shall ever be established by law.

ARTICLE XVIII. Moral qualifications for office; moral obligations of law-givers and magistrates. A frequent recurrence to the fundamental principles of the constitution and a constant adherence to those of piety, justice, moderation, temperance, industry, and frugality, are absolutely necessary to preserve the advantages of liberty, and to maintain a free government. The people ought, consequently, to have a particular attention to all those principles, in the choice of their Officers and Representatives; and they have a right to require of their law-givers and magistrates an exact and constant observance of them, in the formation and execution of the laws necessary for the good administration of the Commonwealth.

ARTICLES OF AMENDMENT

ARTICLE XI. Religious Freedom Established.

"Instead of the Third Article of the Bill of Rights, the following Modification and Amendment thereof is substituted.

As the public worship of God and instructions in piety, religion and morality, promote the happiness and prosperity of a people and the security of a Republican Government;—Therefore, the several religious societies of this Commonwealth, whether corporate or unincorporate, at any meeting legally warned and holden for that purpose, shall ever have the right to elect their pastors or religious teachers, to contract with them for their support, to raise money for erecting and repairing houses for public worship, for the maintenance of religious instruction, and for the payment of necessary expenses; And all persons belonging to any religious society shall be taken and held to be members, until they shall file with the Clerk of such Society, a written notice, declaring the dissolution of their membership, and thenceforth shall not be liable for any grant or contract, which may be thereafter made, or entered into by such society;—And all religious sects and denominations demearr-ing themselves peaceably and as good citizens of the Commonwealth, shall be equally under the protection of the law; and no subordination of any one sect or denomination to another shall ever be established by law."

ARTICLE XLVI. Religious Freedom, Public Money not to be appropriated for Founding, Maintaining or aiding Educational, Charitable or Religious Institutions not publicly owned, care or support of public charges in private hospitals; religious services for inmates of certain institutions.

[In place of article XVIII of the articles of amendment of the constitution ratified and adopted April 9, 1821, the following article of amendment, submitted by the constitutional convention, was ratified and adopted November 6, 1917.]

ARTICLE XVIII. Section 1. No law shall be passed prohibiting the free exercise of religion.

Section 2. All moneys raised by taxation in the towns and cities for the support of public schools, and all moneys which may be appropriated by the commonwealth for the support of common schools shall be applied to, and expended in, no other schools than those which are conducted according to law, under the order and super-intendence of the authorities of the town or city in which the money is expended; and no grant, appropriation or use of public money or property or loan of public credit shall be made or authorized by the commonwealth or any political division thereof for the purpose of founding, maintaining or aiding any school or institution of learning, whether under public control or otherwise, wherein any denominational doctrine is inculcated or any other school, or any college, infirmary, hospital institution, or educational, charitable or religious undertaking which is not publicly owned and under the exclusive control, order and super-intendence of public officers or public agents authorized by the commonwealth, or federal authority or both, except that appropriations may be made for the maintenance and support of the Soldiers' Home in Massachusetts and for free public libraries in any city or town, and to carry out legal obligations, if any, already entered into; and no such grant, appropriation or use of public money or property or loan of public credit shall be made or authorized for the purpose of founding, maintaining or aiding any church, religious denomination or society.

Section 3. Nothing herein contained shall be construed to prevent the commonwealth, or any political division thereof, from paying to privately controlled hospitals, infirmaries, or institutions for the deaf, dumb or blind not more than the ordinary and reasonable compensation for care or support actually rendered or furnished by such hospitals, infirmaries or institutions to such persons as may be in whole or in part unable to support or care for themselves.

Section 4. Nothing herein contained shall be construed to deprive any inmate of a publicly controlled reformatory, panel or charitable institution of the opportunity of religious exercises therein of his own faith; but no inmate of such institution shall be compelled to attend religious services or receive religious instruction against his will, or, if a minor, without the consent of his parent or guardian.

ARTICLE XLVIII. THE INITIATIVE AND REFERENDUM

Section 2. Excluded Matters.—No measure that relates to religion, religious practices or religious institutions: . . . shall be proposed by an initiative petition. . . .

CONSTITUTION OF MICHIGAN
1963

(Effective January 1, 1964)

Preamble. We, the people of the State of Michigan, grateful to Almighty God . . .

ARTICLE I
DECLARATION OF RIGHTS

Equal protection; discrimination. Sec. 2. No person shall be denied the equal protection of the laws; nor shall any person be denied the enjoyment of his civil or political rights or be discriminated against in the exercise thereof because of religion, race, color or national origin. The legislature shall implement this section by appropriate legislation.

Freedom of worship and religious belief; appropriations. Sec. 4. Every person shall be at liberty to worship God according to the dictates of his own conscience. No person shall be compelled to attend, or, against his consent, to contribute to the erection or support of any place of religious worship, or to pay tithes, taxes or other rates for the support of any minister of the gospel or teacher of religion. No money shall be appropriated or drawn from the treasury for the benefit of any religious sect or society, theological or religious seminary; nor shall property belonging to the state be appropriated for any such purpose. The civil and political rights, privileges and capacities of no person shall be diminished or enlarged on acount of his religious belief.

Witness; competency, religious beliefs. Sec. 18. No person shall be rendered incompetent to be a witness on account of his opinions on matters of religious belief.

73

ARTICLE IV
LEGISLATIVE BRANCH

Chaplains in state institutions. Sec. 47. The legislature may authorize the employment of chaplains in state institutions of detention or confinement.

ARTICLE VIII
EDUCATION

Encouragement of education. Sec. 1. Religion, morality and knowledge being necessary to good government and the happiness of mankind, schools and the means of education shall forever be encouraged.

ARTICLE IX
FINANCE AND TAXATION

Exemption of religious or educational nonprofit organizations. Sec. 4. Property owned and occupied by non-profit religious or educational organizations and used exclusively for religious or educational purposes, as defined by law, shall be exempt from real and personal property taxes.

CONSTITUTION OF MINNESOTA
1857
PREAMBLE

We, the people of the State of Minnesota, grateful to God...

ARTICLE I. BILL OF RIGHTS

Sec. 16. Freedom of conscience; no preference to be given to any religious establishment or mode of worship. The enumeration of rights in this constitution shall not be construed to deny or impair others retained by and inherent in the people. The right of every man to worship God according to the dictates of his own conscience shall never be infringed, nor shall any man be compelled to attend, erect or support any place of worship, or to maintain any religious or ecclesiastical ministry, against his consent; nor shall any control of or interference with the rights of conscience be permitted, or any preference be given by law to any religious establishment or mode of worship; but the liberty of conscience hereby secured shall not be so construed as to excuse acts of licentiousness, or justify practices inconsistent with the peace or safety of the State, nor shall any money be drawn from the treasury for the benefit of any religious societies, or religious or theological seminaries.

Sec. 17. No religious test or property qualifications to be required. No religious test or amount of property shall ever be required as a qualification for any office of public trust under the State. No religious test or amount of property shall ever be required as a qualification of any voter at any election in this State; nor shall any person be rendered incompetent to give evidence in any court of law or equity in consequence of his opinion upon the subject of religion.

ARTICLE VIII. SCHOOL FUNDS, EDUCATION AND SCIENCE

Sec. 3. Public schools in each township to be established. The legislature shall make such provisions, by taxation or otherwise, as, with the income arising from the school funds, will secure a thorough and efficient system of public schools in each township in the State.

Prohibition as to aiding sectarian school. But in no case shall the moneys derived as aforesaid, or any portion thereof, or any public moneys or property, be appropriated or used for the support of schools wherein the distinctive doctrines, creeds or tenets of any particular Christian or other religious sect are promulgated or taught.

ARTICLE IX. FINANCES OF THE STATE AND BANKS AND BANKING

Sec. I. Power of taxation; legislature may authorize. The power of taxation shall never be surrendered, suspended or contracted away. Taxes shall be uniform upon the same class of subjects, and shall be levied and collected for public purposes, but public burying grounds, public school houses, public hospitals, academies, colleges, universities and all seminaries of learning, all churches, church property and houses of worship, institutions of purely public charity, and public property used exclusively for any public purpose, shall be exempt from taxation...

CONSTITUTION OF MISSISSIPPI
1890
PREAMBLE

We, the people of Mississippi in convention assembled, grateful to Almighty God, and invoking his blessing on our work...

ARTICLE 3. BILL OF RIGHTS

Sec. 18. Freedom of religion. No religious test as a qualification for office shall be required; and no preference shall be given by law to any religious sect or mode of worship; but the free enjoyment of all religious sentiments and the different modes of worship shall be held sacred. The rights hereby secured shall not be construed to justify acts of licentiousness injurious to morals or dangerous to the peace and safety of the state, or to exclude the Holy Bible from use in any public school of this state.

ARTICLE 4. LEGISLATIVE DEPARTMENT

Sec. 66. Donations by legislature. No law granting a donation or gratuity in favor of any person or object shall be enacted except by the concurrence of two-thirds of the members elect of each branch of the legislature, nor by any vote for a sectarian purpose or use.

Sec. 90. Certain local, private or special laws, prohibited. The legislature shall not pass local, private, or special laws in any of the following enumerated cases, but such matters shall be provided for only by general laws, viz:...

...(p) Providing for the management or support of any private or common school, incorporating the same, or granting such school any privileges;...

...(u) Granting any lands under control of the state to any person or corporation...

ARTICLE 8. EDUCATION

Sec. 208. Sectarian instruction. No religious or other sect or sects shall ever control any part of the school or other educational funds of this state; nor shall any funds be appropriated toward the support of any sectarian school, or to any school that at the time of receiving such appropriation is not conducted as a free school.

ARTICLE XIV. GENERAL PROVISIONS

Sec. 265. Atheists. No person who denies the existence of a Supreme Being shall hold any office in this state.

CONSTITUTION OF MISSOURI
1945
PREAMBLE

We, the people of Missouri with profound reverence for the Supreme Ruler of the Universe, and grateful for His goodness...

ARTICLE I. BILL OF RIGHTS

Sec. 5. Religious freedom; liberty of conscience and belief; limitations. That all men have a natural and indefeasible right to worship Almighty God according to the dictates of their own consciences; that no human authority can control or interfere with the rights of conscience; that no person shall, on account of his religious persuasion or belief, be rendered ineligible to any public office of trust or profit in this state, be disqualified from testifying or serving as a juror, or be molested in his person or estate; but this section shall not be construed to excuse acts of licentiousness, nor to justify practices inconsistent with the good order, peace or safety of the state, or with the rights of others.

Sec. 6. Practice and support of religion not compulsory; contracts therefor enforcible. That no person can be compelled to erect, support or attend any place or system of worship, or to maintain or support any priest, minister, preacher or teacher of any sect, church, creed or denomination of religion; but if any person shall voluntarily make a contract for any such object, he shall be held to the performance of the same.

Sec. 7. Public aid for religious purposes; preferences and discriminations on religious grounds. That no money shall ever be taken from the public treasury, directly or indirectly, in aid of any church, sect or denomination of religion, or in aid of any priest, preacher, minister or teacher thereof, as such; and that no preference shall be given to nor any discrimination made against any church, sect or creed of religion, or any form of religious faith or worship.

ARTICLE III. LEGISLATIVE DEPARTMENT

Sec. 38(a). Limitation on use of state funds and credit; exceptions; public calamity; blind pensions; old-age assistance; aid to children; direct relief; adjusted compensation for veterans; rehabilitation; participation in federal aid. The general assembly shall have no power to grant public money or property, or lend or authorize the lending of public credit, to any private person, association or corporation, excepting aid in public calamity, and general laws providing for pensions for the blind, for old age assistance, for aid to dependent or crippled children or the blind, for direct relief, for adjusted compensation, bonus or rehabilitation for discharged members of the armed services of the United States who were bona fide residents of this state during their service, and for the rehabilitation of other persons...

ARTICLE IX. EDUCATION

Sec. 8. Prohibition of public aid for religious purposes and institutions. Neither the general assembly, nor any county, city, town, township, school district or other municipal corporation, shall ever make an appropriation or pay from any public fund whatever, anything in aid of any religious creed, church or sectarian purpose or to help to support or sustain any private or public school, academy, seminary, college, university, or other institution of learning controlled by any religious creed, church or sectarian denomination whatever; nor shall any grant or donation of personal property or real estate ever be made by the state, or any county, city, town or other municipal corporation, for any religious creed, church, or sectarian purpose whatever.

ARTICLE X. TAXATION

Sec. 6. Exemptions from taxation. All property, real and personal, of the state, counties and other political subdivisions, and non profit cemeteries, shall be exempt from taxation; and all property, real and personal not held for private or corporate profit and used exclusively for religious worship, for schools and colleges, for purposes purely charitable, or for agricultural and horticultural societies may be exempted from taxation by general law. All laws exempting from taxation property other than the property enumerated in this article, shall be void.

CONSTITUTION OF MONTANA
1889
PREAMBLE

We, the people of Montana, grateful to Almighty God...

ARTICLE III. A DECLARATION OF RIGHTS OF THE PEOPLE OF THE STATE OF MONTANA

Sec. 4. Religious freedom. The free exercise and enjoyment of religious profession and worship, without discrimination, shall forever hereafter be guaranteed and no person shall be denied any civil or political right or privilege on account of his opinions concerning religion, but the liberty of conscience hereby shall not be construed to dispense with oaths or affirmations, excuse acts of licentiousness, by bigamous or polygamous marriage, or otherwise, or justify practices inconsistent with the good order, peace, or safety of the state, or opposed to the civil authority thereof, or of the United States. No person shall be required to attend any place of worship or support any ministry, religious sect, or denomination, against his consent; nor shall any preference be given by law to any religious denomination or mode of worship.

ARTICLE V. LEGISLATIVE DEPARTMENT

Sec. 35. Appropriations to private institutions. No appropriation shall be made for charitable, industrial, educational or benevolent purpose to any person, corporation or community not under the absolute control of the state, nor to any denominational or sectarian institution or association.

ARTICLE XI. EDUCATION

Sec. 8. State aid to sectarian schools. Neither the legislative assembly, nor any county, city, town, or school district, or other public corporations, shall ever make directly, or indirectly, any appropriation, or pay from any public fund or moneys whatever, or make any grant of lands or other property in aid of any church, or for any sectarian purpose, or to aid in the support of any school, academy, seminary, college, university, or other literary, scientific institution, controlled in whole or in part by any church, sect or denomination whatever.

Sec. 9. Admission to public schools; religious teaching. No religious or partisan test or qualification shall ever be required of any person as a condition of admission into any public educational institution of the state, either as teacher or student; nor shall attendance be required at any religious service whatever, nor shall any sectarian tenets be taught in any public educational institution of the state; nor shall any person be debarred admission to any of the collegiate departments of the university on account of sex.

ARTICLE XII. REVENUE AND TAXATION

Sec. 2. Property exempt from taxation...and such other property as may be used exclusively for the agricultural and horticultural societies, for educational purposes, places for actual religious worship, hospitals and places of burial not used or held for private or corporate profit, institutions of purely public charity...may be exempt from taxation.

ARTICLE XIII. PUBLIC INDEBTEDNESS

Sec. 1. Prohibition against state and subdivision participation in private enterprises. Neither the state, nor any county, city, town, municipality, nor other subdivisions of the state shall ever give or loan its credit in aid of, or make any donation or grant, by subsidy or otherwise, to any individual, association or corporation, or become a subscriber to, or a share holder in, any company or corporation, or a joint owner with any person, company, or corporation, except as to such ownership as may accrue to the state by operation or provision of law.

ORDINANCE NO. I. FEDERAL RELATIONS

Be It Ordained: First. That perfect toleration of religious sentiment shall be secured and that no inhabitant of the state of Montana shall ever be molested in person or property, on account of his or her mode of religious worship.

Fourth. That provision shall be made for the establishment and maintenance of a uniform system of public schools, which shall be open to all the children of said state of Montana and free from sectarian control.

CONSTITUTION OF NEVADA
1864
ORDINANCE

...freedom of religious worship...lands.

Second. That perfect toleration of religious sentiment shall be secured, and no inhabitant of said state shall ever be molested, in person or property, on account of his or her mode of religious worship.

PREAMBLE

We the people of the State of Nevada Grateful to Almighty God...

ARTICLE I. DECLARATION OF RIGHTS

Sec. 4. Liberty of conscience. The free exercise and enjoyment of religious profession and worship without discrimination or preference shall forever be allowed in this State, and no person shall be rendered incompetent to be a witness on account of his opinions on matters of his religious belief, but the liberty of conscience (conscience) hereby secured, shall not be so construed, as to excuse acts of licentiousness or justify practices inconsistent with the peace, or safety of this State.

ARTICLE 8. MUNICIPAL AND OTHER CORPORATIONS

Sec. 2. Corporate property subject to taxation; exemptions. All real property, and possessory rights to the same, as well as personal property in this State, belonging to corporations now existing or hereafter created shall be subject to taxation, the same as property of individuals; Provided that the property of corporations formed for Municipal, Charitable, Religious, or Educational purposes may be exempted by law.

ARTICLE II. EDUCATION

Sec. 2 Uniform system of common schools. The legislature shall provide for a uniform system of common schools, by which a school shall be established and maintained in each school district at least six months in every year, and any school district which shall allow instruction of a sectarian character therein may be deprived of its proportion of the interest of the public school fund during such neglect or infraction, and the legislature may pass such laws as will tend to secure a general attendance of the children in each school district upon said public schools.

Sec. 9. Sectarian instruction prohibited in common schools, university. No sectarian instruction shall be imparted or tolerated in any school or University that may be established under this Constitution.

Sec. 10. No public funds to be used for sectarian purposes. No public funds of any kind or character whatever, State, County or Municipal, shall be used for sectarian purpose.

CONSTITUTION OF NEW JERSEY
1947

We, the people of the State of New Jersey, grateful to Almighty God for the civil and religious liberty which He hath so long permitted us to enjoy, and looking to Him for a blessing upon our endeavors to secure and transmit the same unimpaired to succeeding generations, do ordain and establish this Constitution.

ARTICLE I. RIGHTS AND PRIVILEGES

3. Rights of conscience; religious freedom. No person shall be deprived of the inestimable privilege of worshipping Almighty God in a manner agreeable to the dictates of his own conscience; nor under any pretense whatever be compelled to attend any place of worship contrary to his faith and judgment; nor shall any person be obliged to pay tithes, taxes, or other rates for building or repairing any church or churches, place or places of worship, or for the maintenance of any minister or ministry, contrary to what he believes to be right or has deliberately and voluntarily engaged to perform.

4. Establishment of religious sect; religious or racial test for public

office. There shall be no establishment of one religious sect in preference to another; no religious or racial test shall be required as a qualification for any office or public trust.

5. Denial of rights; discrimination; segregation. No person shall be denied the enjoyment of any civil or military right, nor be discriminated against in the exercise of any civil or military right, nor be segregated in the militia or in the public schools, because of religious principles, race, color, ancestry or national origin.

ARTICLE IV. LEGISLATIVE
SECTION VII

2. Gambling

B. It shall be lawful for the Legislature to authorize by law, bona fide veterans, charitable, educational, religious or fraternal organizations, civic and service clubs, volunteer fire companies and first-aid or rescue squads to conduct games of chance of, and restricted to, the selling of rights to participate, and the awarding of prizes in the specific kind of games of chance sometimes known as raffles, conducted by the drawing for prizes or by the allotment of prizes by chance, when the entire net proceeds of such games of chance are to be devoted to educational, charitable, patriotic, religious or public-spirited uses, in any municipality, in which such law shall be adopted by a majority of the qualified voters, voting thereon, at a general or special election as the submission thereof shall be prescribed by law and for the Legislature, from time to time, to restrict and control, by law, the conduct of such games of chance.

ARTICLE VIII. TAXATION AND FINANCE
SECTION I

2. Taxation; exemptions, in general. Exemption from taxation may be granted only by general laws. Until otherwise provided by law all exemptions from taxation validly granted and now in existence shall be continued. Exemptions from taxation may be altered or repealed, except those exempting real and personal property used exclusively for religious, educational, charitable or cemetery purposes, as defined by law, and owned by any corporation or association organized and conducted exclusively for one or more of such purposes and not operating for profit.

SECTION III

3. Donations of land and appropriations of money to private agencies. No donation of land or appropriation of money shall be made by the State or any county or municipal corporation to or for the use of any society, association or corporation whatever.

3. Transportation of school children. The Legislature may, within reasonable limitations as to distance to be prescribed, provide for the transportation of children within the ages of five to eighteen years inclusive, to and from any school.

CONSTITUTION OF NEW MEXICO
1913
PREAMBLE

We, the people of New Mexico, grateful to Almighty God...

ARTICLE II. BILL OF RIGHTS

Sec. 5. Rights under treaty of Guadalupe Hidalgo preserved. The rights, privileges and immunities, civil, political and religious, guaranteed to the people of New Mexico by the treaty of Guadalupe Hidalgo shall be preserved inviolate.

Sec. 11. Freedom of religion. Every man shall be free to worship God according to the dictates of his own conscience, and no person shall ever be molested or denied any civil or political right or privilege on account of his religious opinion or mode of religious worship. No person shall be required to attend any place of worship or support any religious sect or denomination; nor shall any preference be given by law to any religious denomination or mode of worship.

ARTICLE IV. LEGISLATIVE DEPARTMENT

Sec. 31. Aid to charities. No appropriation shall be made for charitable, educational or other benevolent purposes to any person, corporation, association, institution or community, not under the absolute control of the state, but the legislature may, in its discretion, make appropriations for the charitable institutions and hospitals, for the maintenance of which annual appropriations were made by the legislative assembly of nineteen hundred and nine.

ARTICLE VII. ELECTIVE FRANCHISE

Sec. 3. Religious and racial equality protected; restrictions on amendments. The right of any citizen of the state to vote, hold office, or sit upon juries, shall never be restricted, abridged or impaired on account of religion, race, language or color, or inability to speak, read or write the English or Spanish languages except as may be otherwise provided in this Constitution...

ARTICLE VIII. TAXATION AND REVENUE

Sec. 3. Tax exempt property . . . all church property, all property used for educational or charitable purposes, all cemeteries not used or held for private or corporate profit...shall be exempt from taxation.

Provided, however, that any...property acquired by churches, property acquired and used for educational or charitable purposes, where such property was, prior to such transfer, subject to the lien of any tax or assessment for the principal or interest of any bonded indebtedness shall not be exempt from such lien, nor from the payment of such taxes or assessments.

ARTICLE IX. STATE, COUNTY AND MUNICIPAL INDEBTEDNESS

Sec. 14. Aid to private enterprise. Neither the state, nor any county, school district, or municipality, except as otherwise provided in this Constitution, shall directly or indirectly lend or pledge its credit, or make any donation to or in aid of any person, association, or public or private corporation, or in aid of any private enterprise for the construction of any railroad; provided, nothing herein shall be construed to prohibit the State or any county or municipality from making provision for the care and maintenance of sick and indigent persons.

ARTICLE XII. EDUCATION

Sec. 3. Control of educational institutions provided for in constitution; use of state land proceeds. The schools, colleges, universities and other educational institutions provided for by this Constitution shall forever remain under the exclusive control of the State, and no part of the proceeds arising from the sale or disposal of any lands granted to the State by Congress, or any other funds appropriated, levied or collected for educational purposes, shall be used for the support of any sectarian, denominational or private school, college or university.

Sec. 9. Religious tests in schools. No religious test shall ever be required as a condition of admission into the public schools or any educational institution of this State, either as a teacher or student and no teacher or students of such school or institution shall ever be required to attend or participate in any religious service whatsoever.

ARTICLE XX. MISCELLANEOUS

Sec. 13. Sacramental wines. The use of wines solely for sacramental purposes under church authority at any place within the state shall never be prohibited.

ARTICLE XXI. COMPACT WITH THE UNITED STATES

Sec. 1. Religious toleration; polygamy. Perfect toleration of religious sentiment shall be secured, and no inhabitant of this state shall ever be molested in person or property on account of his or her mode of religious worship. Polygamous or plural marriages and polygamous cohabitation are forever prohibited.

83

Sec. 4. Public Schools. Provision shall be made for the establishment and maintenance of a system of public schools which shall be open to all the children of the State and free from sectarian control, and said schools shall always be conducted in English.

CONSTITUTION OF NEW YORK
1895
PREAMBLE

We, the people of the State of New York, grateful to Almighty God.

ARTICLE I. BILL OF RIGHTS

Sec. 3. Freedom of worship; religious liberty. The free exercise and enjoyment of religious profession and worship, without discrimination or preference, shall forever be allowed in this state to all mankind; and no person shall be rendered incompetent to be a witness on account of his opinions on matters of religious belief; but the liberty of conscience hereby secured shall not be so construed as to excuse acts of licentiousness, or justify practices inconsistent with the peace or safety of this state.

Sec. 11. Equal protection of laws; discrimination in civil rights prohibited. No person shall be denied the equal protection of the laws of this state or any subdivision thereof. No person shall, because of race, color, creed or religion, be subjected to any discrimination in his civil rights by any other person or by any firm, corporation, or institution, or by the state or any agency or subdivision of the state.

ARTICLE VII. STATE FINANCE

Sec. 8. Gift or loan of state credit or money prohibited; exceptions for enumerated purposes. The money of the state shall not be given or loaned to or in aid of any private corporation or association, or private undertaking; nor shall the credit of the state be given or loaned to or in aid of any individual, or public or private corporation or association, or private undertaking, but the foregoing provisions shall not apply to any fund or property now held or which may hereafter be held by the state for educational purposes.

Subject to the limitations on indebtedness and taxation, nothing in this constitution contained shall prevent the legislature from providing for the aid, care and support of the needy directly or through subdivisions of the state; or for the protection by insurance or otherwise, against the hazards of unemployment, sickness and old age; or for the education and support of the blind, the deaf, the dumb, the physically handicapped and juvenile delinquents as it may deem proper; or for health and welfare services for all children, either directly or through subdivisions of the state, incuding school districts; or for the aid, care and support of neglected and dependent children and of the needy sick through agencies and institutions authorized by the state board of social welfare or other state department having the power of inspection thereof, by payments made on a per capita basis directly or through the subdivisions of the state; or for the increase in the amount of pensions of any member of a retirement system of the state, or of a subdivision of the state. The enumeration of legislative powers in this paragraph shall not be taken to diminish any power of the legislature hitherto existing.

ARTICLE VIII. LOCAL FINANCES

Sec. 1. Gift or loan of property or credit of local subdivisions prohibited; exceptions for enumerated purposes...

Subject to the limitations on indebtedness and taxation applying to any county, city or town, nothing in this constitution contained shall prevent a county, city or town from making such provision for the aid, care and support of the needy as may be authorized by law, nor prevent any such county, city or town from providing for the care, support, maintenance and secular education of inmates of orphan asylums, homes for dependent children or correctional institutions and of children placed in family homes by authorized agencies, whether under public or private control. . . .

Payments by counties, cities or towns to charitable, eleemosynary, correctional and reformatory institutions and agencies, wholly or partly under private control, for care, support and maintenance may be authorized, but shall not be required by the legislature. . . .

ARTICLE XI. EDUCATION

Sec. 3. Use of public property or money in aid of denominational schools prohibited; transportation of children authorized. Neither the state nor any subdivision thereof shall use its property or credit or any public money, or authorize or permit either to be used, directly or indirectly, in aid of maintenance, other than for examination or inspection, of any school or institution of learning wholly or in part under the control or direction of any religious denomination, or in which any denominational tenet or doctrine is taught, but the legislature may provide for the transportation of children to and from any school or institution of learning.

. ARTICLE XVI. TAXATION

Sec. 1. . . . exemptions from taxation. . . .

Exemptions from taxation may be granted only by general laws. Exemptions may be altered or repealed except those exempting real or personal property used exclusively for religious, educational or charitable purposes as defined by law and owned by any corporation or association organized or conducted exclusively for one or more of such purposes and not operating for profit.

CONSTITUTION OF NORTH CAROLINA
1868
PREAMBLE

We, the people of the State of North Carolina, grateful to Almighty God, the Sovereign Ruler of Nations...and acknowledging our dependence upon Him for the continuance of those blessings to us and our posterity...

ARTICLE I. DECLARATION OF RIGHTS

Sec. 26. Religious liberty. All persons have a natural and inalienable right to worship Almighty God according to the dictates of their own consciences, and no human authority should, in any case whatever, control or interfere with the rights of conscience.

ARTICLE V. REVENUE AND TAXATION

Sec. 5. Property exempt from taxation. Property belonging to the State or to municipal corporations, shall be exempt from taxation. The General Assembly may exempt cemeteries and property held for educational, scientific, literary, charitable, or religious purposes;...

ARTICLE VI. SUFFRAGE AND ELIGIBILITY TO OFFICE

Sec. 8. Disqualification for office. The following classes of persons shall be disqualified for office: first, all persons who shall deny the being of Almighty God...

ARTICLE IX. EDUCATION

Sec. 1. Education shall be encouraged. Religion, morality, and knowledge being necessary to good government and the happiness of mankind, schools and the means of education shall forever be encouraged.

ARTICLE XI. PUNISHMENTS, PENAL INSTITUTIONS, AND PUBLIC CHARITIES

Sec. 7. Provision for the poor and orphans. Beneficent provisions for the poor, the unfortunate and orphan, being one of the first duties of a civilized and Christian state, the General Assembly shall, at its first session, appoint and define the duties of a board of public charities, to whom shall be entrusted the supervision of all charitable and penal State institutions, and who shall annually report to the Governor upon their condition, with suggestions for their improvement.

ARTICLE XII. MILITIA

Sec. 1. Who are liable to militia duty. All able-bodied male citizens of the State of North Carolina, between the ages of twenty-one and forty years, who are citizens of the United States, shall be liable to duty in the militia: Provided, that all persons who may be averse to bearing arms, from religious scruples, shall be exempt therefrom.

CONSTITUTION OF NORTH DAKOTA
1889

We, the people of North Dakota, grateful to Almighty God...

ARTICLE I. DECLARATION OF RIGHTS

Sec. 4. Religious freedom. The free exercise and enjoyment of religious profession and worship, without discrimination or preference, shall be forever guaranteed in this state, and no person shall be rendered incompetent to be a witness or juror on account of his opinion on matters of religious belief; but the liberty of conscience hereby secured shall not be so construed as to excuse acts of licentiousness, or justify practices inconsistent with the peace or safety of this state.

ARTICLE VIII. EDUCATION

Sec. 147. Public schools. A high degree of intelligence, patriotism, integrity and morality on the part of every voter in a government by the people being necessary in order to insure the continuance of that government and the prosperity and happiness of the people, the legislative assembly shall make provision for the establishment and maintenance of a system of public schools which shall be open to all children of the state of North Dakota and free from sectarian control. This legislative requirement shall be irrevocable without the consent of the United States and the people of North Dakota.

Sec. 149. Moral instruction. In all schools instruction shall be given as far as practicable in those branches of knowledge that tend to impress upon the mind the vital importance of truthfulness, temperance, purity, public spirit, and respect for honest labor of every kind.

Sec. 152. Support of private schools. All colleges, universities, and other educational institutions, for the support of which lands have been granted to this state, or which are supported by a public tax, shall remain under the absolute and exclusive control of the state. No money raised for the support of the public schools of the state shall be appropriated to or used for the support of any sectarian school.

ARTICLE IX. SCHOOL AND PUBLIC LANDS

Sec. 158. Sale of school lands. . . .

Any said lands that may be required for...school house sites, church sites, cemetery sites, sites for other educational or charitable institutions...or for any of the purposes for which private lands may be taken under the right of eminent domain under the Constitution and laws of this state, may be sold under the provisions of this Article, and shall be paid for in full at the time of sale, or at any time thereafter as herein provided...

ARTICLE XI. REVENUE AND TAXATION

Sec. 176. Exemptions....and property used exclusively for schools, religious, cemetery, charitable or other purposes shall be exempt from taxation. . . .

ARTICLE XII. PUBLIC DEBT AND PUBLIC WORKS

Sec. 185. Internal improvements. . . . neither the state nor any political subdivision thereof shall otherwise loan or give its credit or make donations to or in aid of any individual, association or corporation except for reasonable support of the poor, nor subscribe to or become the owner of capital stock in any association or corporation.

ARTICLE XIII. MILITIA

Sec. 188. Composition. The militia of this state shall consist of all able-bodied male persons residing in the state, between the ages of eighteen and forty-five years, except such as may be exempted by the laws of the United States or of this state. Persons whose religious tenets or conscientious scruples forbid them to bear arms shall not be compelled to do so in times of peace, but shall pay an equivalent for a personal service.

ARTICLE XVI. COMPACT WITH THE UNITED STATES

Sec. 203. First. Religious liberty. Perfect toleration of religious sentiment shall be secured, and no inhabitant of this state shall ever be molested in person or property on account of his or her mode of religious worship. . . .

ARTICLE XVII. MISCELLANEOUS

Sec. 211. Oath of office. Members of the legislative assembly and judicial departments, except of such inferior officers as may be by law exempted shall before they enter on the duties of their respective offices, take and subscribe the following oath or affirmation: "I do solemnly swear (or affirm as the case may be) that I will support the constitution of the United States and the constitution of the state of North Dakota; and that I will faithfully discharge the duties of the office of........ . . . according to the best of my ability, so help me God" (if an oath), (under pains and penalties of perjury) if an affirmation, and no other oath, declaration, or test shall be required as a qualification for any office or public trust.

CONSTITUTION OF OHIO
1851
PREAMBLE

We, the people of the State of Ohio, grateful to Almighty God...

ARTICLE I. BILL OF RIGHTS

Sec. 7. Rights of conscience; the necessity of religion and knowledge. All men have a natural and indefeasible right to worship Almighty God according to the dictates of their own conscience. No person shall be compelled to attend, erect, or support any place of worship, or maintain any form of worship, against his consent; and no preference shall be given, by law, to any religious society; nor shall any interference with the rights of conscience be permitted. No religious test shall be required, as a qualification for office, nor shall any person be incompetent to be a witness on account of his religious belief; but nothing herein shall be construed to dispense with oaths and affirmations. Religion, morality, and knowledge, however, being essential to good government, it shall be the duty of the General Assembly to pass suitable laws, to protect every religious denomination in the peaceable enjoyment of its own mode of public worship, and to encourage schools and the means of instruction.

ARTICLE VI. EDUCATION

Sec. 1. Funds for educational and religious purposes. The principal of all funds, arising from the sale, or other disposition of lands, or other property, granted or entrusted to this State for educational and religious purposes, shall forever be preserved inviolate, and undiminished; and, the income arising therefrom, shall be faithfully applied to the specific objects of the original grants, or appropriations.

Sec. 2. Common school fund to be raised; how controlled. The General Assembly shall make such provisions, by taxation, or otherwise, as, with the income arising from the school trust fund, will secure a thorough and efficient system of common schools throughout the State; but, no religious or other sect, or sects, shall ever have any exclusive right to, or control of, any part of the school funds of this State.

ARTICLE VII. FINANCE AND TAXATION

Sec. 2. Taxation by uniform rule; exemption. . . . general laws may be passed to exempt burying grounds, public school houses, houses used exclusively for public worship, institutions used exclusively for charitable purposes and public property used exclusively for any public purpose, but all such laws shall be subject to alteration or repeal;...

CONSTITUTION OF PENNSYLVANIA
1874
PREAMBLE

We, the people of the Commonwealth of Pennsylvania, grateful to Almighty God...and humbly invoking His guidance...

ARTICLE I. DECLARATION OF RIGHTS

Sec. 3. Rights of conscience; freedom of religious worship. All men have a natural and indefeasible right to worship Almighty God according to the dictates of their own consciences; no man can of right be compelled to attend, erect or support any place of worship, or to maintain any ministry against his consent; no human authority can, in any case whatever, control or interfere with the rights of conscience and no preference shall ever be given by law to any religious establishment or modes of worship.

Sec. 4. No disqualification for religious belief. No person who acknowledges the being of a God, and a future state of rewards and punishments shall, on account of his religious sentiments, be disqualified to hold any office or place of trust or profit under this Commonwealth.

ARTICLE III. LEGISLATION

Sec. 17. Appropriations to charitable and educational institutions. No appropriation shall be made to any charitable or educational institution not under the absolute control of the Commonwealth, other than normal schools established by law for the professional training of teachers for the public schools of the State, except by a vote of two-thirds of all the members elected to each House.

Sec. 18. Certain appropriations forbidden. No appropriations shall be made for charitable, educational or benevolent purposes to any person or community nor to any denominational and sectarian institution, corporation or association; Provided, that appropriations may be made for pensions or gratuities for military services, and to blind persons twenty-one years of age and upwards, and for assistance to mothers having dependent children, and to aged persons, without adequate means of support.

ARTICLE IX. TAXATION AND FINANCE

Sec. 1. Taxes to be uniform; exemptions. All taxes shall be uniform, upon the same class of subjects, within the territorial limits of the authority levying the tax, and shall be levied and collected under general laws; but the General Assembly may, by general laws, exempt from taxation public property used for public purposes, actual places of religious worship, places of burial not used or held for private or corporate profit, and institutions of purely public charity. . . .

ARTICLE X. EDUCATION

Sec. 2. Diversion of school moneys to sectarian schools. No money raised for the support of the public schools of the Commonwealth shall be appropriated to or used for the support of any sectarian school.

ARTICLE XI. MILITIA

Sec. 1. Militia to be organized; maintenance; exemption from service. The freeman of this Commonwealth shall be armed, organized and disciplined for its defense when and in such manner as may be directed by law. The General Assembly shall provide for maintaining the militia by appropriations from the Treasury of the Commonwealth, and may exempt from military service persons having conscientious scruples against bearing arms.

CONSTITUTION OF RHODE ISLAND
1843

We, the people of the State of Rhode Island and Providence Plantations, grateful to Almighty God for the civil and religious liberty which He hath so long permitted us to enjoy, and looking to Him for a blessing upon our endeavors...

ARTICLE I. DECLARATION OF CERTAIN CONSTITUTIONAL RIGHTS AND PRINCIPLES

Sec. 3. Religious freedom secured. Whereas Almighty God hath created the mind free; and all attempts to influence it by temporal punishments or burdens, or by civil incapacitations, tend to beget habits of hypocrisy and meanness; and whereas a principal object of our venerable ancestors, in their migration to this country and their settlement of this state, was as they expresed it, to hold forth a lively experiment, that a flourishing civil state may stand and be best maintained with full liberty in religious concernments: We, therefore, declare that no man shall be compelled to frequent or to support any religious worship, place, or ministry whatever, except in fulfillment of his own voluntary contract; nor enforced, restrained, molested, or burdened in his body or goods; nor disqualified from holding any office; nor otherwise suffer on account of his religious belief; and that every man shall be free to worship God according to the dictates of his own conscience, and to profess and by argument to maintain his opinion in matters of religion; and that the same shall in no wise diminish, enlarge or affect his civil capacity.

CONSTITUTION OF TEXAS
1876
PREAMBLE

Humbly invoking the blessing of Almighty God, the people of the State of Texas, do ordain and establish this Constitution.

ARTICLE I. BILL OF RIGHTS

Sec. 4. No religious test for office. No religious test shall ever be required as a qualification to any office, or public trust, in this State; nor shall anyone be excluded from holding office on account of his religious sentiments provided he acknowledge the existence of a Supreme Being.

Sec. 5. How oaths shall be administered. No person shall be disqualified to give evidence in any of the Courts of this State, on account of his religious opinion, or for the want of any religious belief, but all oaths or affirmations shall be administered in the mode most binding upon the conscience, and shall be taken subject to the pains and penalties of perjury.

Sec. 6. Freedom in religious worship guaranteed. All men have a natural and indefeasible right to worship Almighty God according to the dictates of their own consciences. No man shall be compelled to attend, erect or support any place or worship, or to maintain any ministry against his consent. No human authority ought, in any case whatever, to control or interfere with the rights of conscience in matters of religion, and no preference shall ever be given by law to any religious society or mode of worship. But it shall be the duty of the Legislature to pass such laws as may be necessary to protect equally every religious denomination in the peaceable enjoyment of its own mode of public worship.

Sec. 7. No appropriation for sectarian purposes. No money shall be appropriated, or drawn from the Treasury for the benefit of any sect, or religious society, theological or religious seminary; nor shall property belonging to the State be appropriated for any such purposes.

ARTICLE III. LEGISLATIVE DEPARTMENT

Sec. 51-a. Assistance to needy aged, needy blind, and needy children; limitation on annual expenditures for same. The Legislature shall have the power, by General Laws, to provide, subject to limitations and restrictions herein contained, and such other limitations, restrictions and regulations as may by the Legislature be deemed expedient for assistance to, and for the payment of assistance to:

(1) Needy aged persons who are actual bona fide citizens of Texas and who are over the age of sixty-five (65) years: . . .

(2) Needy blind persons who are actual bona fide citizens of Texas and are over the age of twenty-one (21) years; . . .

(3) Needy children who are actual bona fide citizens of Texas and are under the age of sixteen (16) years; . . .

ARTICLE VII. EDUCATION — THE PUBLIC FREE SCHOOLS

Sec. 5. Permanent school fund; interest; alienation; sectarian schools. . . . And no law shall ever be enacted appropriating any part of the permanent or available school fund to any other purpose whatever; nor shall the same, or any part thereof ever be appropriated to or used for the support of any sectarian school; . . .

ARTICLE VIII. TAXATION AND REVENUE

Sec. 2. . . . exemptions. . . . but the legislature may, by general laws, exempt from taxation, public property used for public purposes; actual places of religious worship, also any property owned by a church or by strictly religious society for the exclusive use as a dwelling place for the ministry of such church or religious society, and which yields no revenue whatever to such church or religious society; provided that such exemption shall not extend to more property than is reasonably necessary for a dwelling place and in no event more than one acre of land; places of burial not held for private or corporate profit; all buildings used exclusively and owned by persons or associations of persons for school purposes and the necessary furniture of all schools and property used exclusively and reasonably necessary in conducting any association engaged in promoting the religious, educational and physical development of boys, girls, young men or young women operating under a State or National organization of like character; also the endowment funds of such institutions of learning and religion not used with a view to profit; . . .

ARTICLE XVI. GENERAL PROVISIONS

Sec. 47. Scruples against bearing arms. Any person who conscientiously scruples to bear arms, shall not be compelled to do so, but shall pay an equivalent for personal service.

CONSTITUTION OF UTAH
1896
PREAMBLE

Grateful to Almighty God for life and liberty, we, the people of Utah, in order to secure and perpetuate the principles of free government, do ordain and establish this CONSTITUTION.

ARTICLE I. DECLARATION OF RIGHTS

Sec. 1. Inherent and inalienable rights. All men have the inherent and inalienable right to enjoy and defend their lives and liberties; to acquire, possess and protect property; to worship according to the dictates of their consciences; to assemble peaceably, protest against wrongs, and petition for redress of grievances; to communicate freely their thoughts and opinions, being responsible for the abuse of that right.

Sec. 4. Religious liberty. The rights of conscience shall never be infringed. The State shall make no law respecting an establishment of religion or prohibiting the free exercise thereof; no religious test shall be required as a qualification for any office of public trust or for any vote at any election; nor shall any person be incompetent as a witness or juror on account of religious belief or the absence thereof. There shall be no union of Church and State, nor shall any church dominate the State or interfere with its functions. No public money or property shall be appropriated for or applied to any religious worship, exercise or instruction, or for the support of any ecclesiastical establishment. No property qualification shall be required of any person to vote, or hold office, except as provided in this Constitution.

ARTICLE III. ORDINANCE

First: —Religious toleration; polygamy forbidden. Perfect toleration of religious sentiment is guaranteed. No inhabitant of this State shall ever be molested in person or property on account of his or her mode of religious worship; but polygamous or plural marriages are forever prohibited.

Fourth: —Free, nonsectarian schools. The Legislature shall make laws for the establishment and maintenance of a system of public schools, which shall be open to all the children of the State and be free from sectarian control.

ARTICLE X. EDUCATION

Sec. 1. Free nonsectarian schools. The Legislature shall provide for the establishment of a uniform system of public schools, which shall be open to all children of the State, and be free from sectarian control.

Sec. 12. No religious or partisan tests in schools. Neither religious nor partisan test or qualification shall be required of any person as a condition of admission, as teacher or student, into any public educational institution of the State.

Sec. 13. Public aid to church schools, forbidden. Neither the Legislature nor any county, city, town, school district or other public corporation, shall make any appropriation to aid in the support of any school, seminary, academy, college, university or other institution, controlled in whole, or in part, by any church, sect or denomination whatever.

ARTICLE XIII. REVENUE AND TAXATION

Sec. 2. Tangible property to be taxed; value ascertained; properties exempt; legislature to provide annual tax for state. All tangible property in the state, not exempt under the laws of the United States, or under this constitution, shall be taxed in proporation to its value, to be ascertained as provided by law. The property of the state, counties, cities, towns, school districts, municipal corporations and public libraries, lots with the buildings thereon used exclusively for either religious worship or charitable purposes, and places of burial not held or used for private or corporate benefit, shall be exempt from taxation. . . .

CONSTITUTION OF VERMONT
1793

CHAPTER I. A DECLARATION OF THE RIGHTS OF THE INHABITANTS OF THE STATE OF VERMONT

Art. 3rd. Religious freedom and worship. That all men have a natural and unalienable right, to worship Almighty God, according to the dictates of their own consciences and understandings, as in their opinion shall be regulated by the word of God; and that no man ought to, or of right can be compelled to attend any religious worship, or erect or support any place of worship, or maintain any minister, contrary to the dictates of his conscience, nor can any man be justly deprived or abridged of any civil right as a citizen, on account of his religious sentiments, or peculia(r) mode of religious worship; and that no authority can, or ought to be vested in, or assumed by, any power whatever, that shall in any case interfere with, or in any manner control the rights of conscience, in the free exercise of religious worship. Nevertheless, every sect or denomination of christians ought to observe the sabbath or Lord's day, and keep up some sort of religious worship, which to them shall seem most agreeable to the revealed will of God.

Art. 9th. Citizens' rights and duties in the state; bearing arms; taxation. That every member of society hath a right to be protected in the enjoyment of life, liberty, and property, and therefor is bound to contribute his proportion towards the expense of that protection, and yield his personal service, when necessary, or an equivalent thereto, but no part of any person's property can be justly taken from him, or applied to public uses, without his own consent, or that of the Representative Body of the freemen, nor can any man who is conscientiously scrupulous of bearing arms, be justly compelled thereto, if he will pay such equivalent; . . .

CHAPTER II. PLAN OR FRAME OF GOVERNMENT

Sec. 64. Laws to encourage virtue and prevent vice; schools; religious socities. Laws for the encouragement of virtue and prevention of vice and immorality, ought to be constantly kept in force, and duly executed; and a competent number of schools ought to be maintained in each town, or by towns jointly with the consent of the General Assembly, for the convenient instruction of youth. All religious societies, or bodies of men that may be united or incorporated for the advancement of religion and learning, or for other pious and charitable purposes, shall be encouraged and protected in the enjoyment of the privileges, immunities, and estates, which they in justice ought to enjoy, under such regulations as the General Assembly of this State shall direct.

CONSTITUTION OF VIRGINIA
1902

ARTICLE I. BILL OF RIGHTS

Sec. 16. Religious freedom. That religion or the duty which we owe to our Creator, and the manner of discharging it, can be directed only by reason and conviction, not by force or violence; and, therefore, all men are equally entitled to the free exercise of religion, according to the dictates of conscience; and that it is the mutual duty of all to practice Christian forbearance, love and charity towards each other.

ARTICLE IV. LEGISLATIVE DEPARTMENT

Sec. 58. Prohibitions on general assembly as to suspension of writ of habeas corpus, and enactment of laws referring to religion and other laws. . . .

No man shall be compelled to frequent or support any religious worship, place or ministry, whatsoever, nor shall be enforced, restrained, molested, or burthened in his body or goods, nor shall otherwise suffer on account of his religious opinions or belief; but all men shall be free to profess and by argument to maintain their opinions in matters of religion, and the same shall in no wise diminish, enlarge, or affect, their civil capacities. And the General Assembly shall not prescribe any religious test whatever, or confer any peculiar privilege or advantages on any sect or denomination, or pass any law requiring or authorizing any religious society, or the people of any district within this State, to levy on themselves, or others, any tax for the erection or repair of any house of public worship, or for the support of any church or ministry; but it shall be left free to every person to select his religious instructor, and to make for his support such private contract as he shall please.

Sec. 59. General assembly shall not incorporate churches or religious denominations; may secure church property. The General Assembly shall not grant a charter of incorporation to any church or religious denomination, but may secure the title to church property to an extent to be limited by law.

Sec. 67. Limitations on appropriations by general assembly to charitable and other institutions; exceptions. The General Assembly shall not make any appropriation of public funds, or personal property, or of any real estate, to any church, or sectarian society, association, or institution of any kind whatever, which is entirely or partly, directly or indirectly, controlled by any church or sectarian society; nor shall the General Assembly make any like appropriation to any charitable institution which is not owned or controlled by the State; except that it may, in its discretion, make appropriation to nonsectarian institutions for the reform of youthful criminals; but nothing herein contained shall prohibit the General Assembly from authorizing counties, cities, or towns to make such appropriations to any charitable institution or association.

ARTICLE IX. EDUCATION AND PUBLIC INSTRUCTION

Sec. 141. State appropriations prohibited to schools or institutions of learning not owned or exclusively controlled by the state or some subdivision thereof; exceptions to rule. No appropriation of public funds shall be made to any school or institution of learning not owned or exclusively controlled by the State or some political subdivision thereof; provided, first that the General Assembly may, and the governing bodies of the several counties, cities and towns, may, subject to such limitations as may be imposed by the General Assembly, appropriate funds for educational purposes which may be expended in furtherance of elementary, secondary, collegiate or graduate education of Virginia students in public and nonsectarian private schools and institutions of learning, in addition to those owned or exclusively controlled by the State or any such county, city or town; second, that the General Assembly may appropriate funds to an agency, or to a school or institution of learning owned or controlled by an agency, created and established by two or more States under a joint agreement to which this State is a party for the purpose of providing educational facilities for the citizens of the several States joining such agreement; third, that counties, cities, towns, and districts may make appropriations to nonsectarian schools of manual, industrial or technical training, and also to any school or institution of learning owned or exclusively controlled by such county, city, town, or school district.

ARTICLE XIII. TAXATION AND FINANCE

Sec. 183. Property exempt from taxation. Unless otherwise provided in this Constitution, the following property and no other shall be exempt from taxation, State and local, including inheritance taxes: . . .

(b) Buildings with land they actually occupy, and the furniture and furnishings therein and endowment funds lawfully owned and held by churches or religious bodies, and wholly and exclusively used for religious worship, or for the residence of the minister of any such church or religious body, together with the additional adjacent land reasonably necessary for the convenient use of any such building. . . .

(e) Real estate belonging to, actually and exclusively occupied and used by, and personal property, including endowment funds, belonging to Young Men's Christian Associations, and other similar religious associations, orphan or other asylums, reformatories, hospitals and nunneries, conducted not for profit, but exclusively as charities, . . .

CONSTITUTION OF WASHINGTON
1889
PREAMBLE

We the people of the State of Washington, grateful to the Supreme Ruler of the Universe for our liberties, do ordain this constitution.

ARTICLE I. DECLARATION OF RIGHTS

Sec. 11. Religious freedom. Absolute freedom of conscience in all matters of religious sentiment, belief and worship, shall be guaranteed to every individual, and no one shall be molested or disturbed in person or property on account of religion; but the liberty of conscience hereby secured shall not be so construed as to excuse acts of licentiousness or justify practices inconsistent with the peace and safety of the state. No public money or property shall be appropriated for or applied to any religious worship, exercise or instruction, or the support of any religious establishment; Provided, however, That this article shall not be so construed as to forbid the employment by the state of a chaplain for such of the state custodial, correctional and mental institutions as in the discretion of the legislature may seem justified. No religious qualification shall be required for any public office or employment, nor shall any person be incompetent as a witness or juror, in consequence of his opinion on matters of religion, nor be questioned in any court of justice touching his religious belief to affect the weight of his testimony.

ARTICLE IX.   EDUCATION

Sec. 4.   Sectarian control or influence prohibited. All schools maintained or supported wholly or in part by the public funds shall be forever free from sectarian control or influence.

ARTICLE X.   MILITIA

Sec. 6.   Exemption from military duty. No person or persons, having conscientious scruples against bearing arms, shall be compelled to do militia duty in time of peace, Provided, such person or persons shall pay an equivalent for such exemption.

ARTICLE XXVI.   COMPACT WITH THE UNITED STATES

First: That perfect toleration of religious sentiment shall be secured and that no inhabitant of this state shall ever be molested in person or property on account of his or her mode of religious worship.

Fourth.   Provision shall be made for the establishment and maintenance of systems of public schools free from sectarian control which shall be open to all the children of said state.

CONSTITUTION OF WEST VIRGINIA
1872
PREAMBLE

Since through Divine Providence we enjoy the blessings of civil, political and religious liberty, we the people of West Virginia, in and through the provisions of this Constitution, reaffirm our faith in and constant reliance upon God and seek diligently to promote, preserve and perpetuate good government in the State of West Virginia for the common welfare, freedom and security of ourselves and our posterity.

ARTICLE III.   BILL OF RIGHTS

11.   Political tests condemned. Political tests, requiring persons, as a prerequisite to the enjoyment of their civil and political rights, to purge themselves by their own oaths, of past alleged offenses, are repugnant to the principles of free government, and are cruel and oppressive. No religious or political test oath shall be required as a prerequisite or qualification to vote, serve as a juror, sue, plead, appeal, or pursue any

profession or employment. Nor shall any person be deprived by law of any right or privilege, because of any act done prior to the passage of such law.

15. Religious freedom guaranteed. No man shall be compelled to frequent or support any religious worship, place or ministry whatsoever, nor shall any man be enforced, restrained, molested or burthened, in his body or goods or otherwise suffer, on account of his religious opinions or belief, but all men shall be free to profess, and, by argument, to maintain their opinions in matters of religion; and the same shall, in no wise, affect, diminish, or enlarge their civil capacities; and the legislature shall not prescribe any religious test whatever, or confer any peculiar privileges or advantages on any sect or denomination, or pass any law requiring or authorizing any religious society, or the people of any district within this State, to levy on themselves, or others any tax for the erection or repair of any house for public worship, or for the support of any church or ministry, but it shall be left free for every person to select his religious instructor, and to make for his support such private contract as he shall please.

ARTICLE VI. LEGISLATURE

Sec. 47. Incorporation of religious denominations prohibited. No charter of incorporation shall be granted to any church or religious denomination. Provisions may be made by general laws for securing the title to church property, and for the sale and transfer thereof, so that it shall be held, used, or transferred for the purposes of such church, or religious denomination.

CONSTITUTION OF WYOMING
1890
PREAMBLE

We, the people of the state of Wyoming, grateful to God for our civil, political and religious liberties, and desiring to secure them to ourselves and perpetuate them to our posterity, do ordain and establish this constitution.

ARTICLE I. DECLARATION OF RIGHTS

Sec. 18. Religious liberty. The free exercise and enjoyment of religious profession and worship without discrimination or preference shall be forever guaranteed in this state, and no person shall be rendered incompetent to hold any office of trust or profit, or to serve as a witness or juror, because of his opinion on any matter of religious belief whatever; but the liberty of conscience hereby secured shall not be so construed as to excuse acts of licentiousness or justify practices inconsistent with the peace or safety of the state.

Sec. 19. Appropriations for religious societies prohibited. No money of the state shall ever be given or appropriated to any sectarian or religious society or institution.

ARTICLE III. LEGISLATIVE DEPARTMENT

Sec. 36. Prohibited appropriations. No appropriation shall be made for charitable, industrial, educational or benevolent purposes to any person, corporation or community not under the absolute control of the state, nor to any denominational or sectarian institution or association.

ARTICLE VII. EDUCATION

Sec. 8. Distribution of school funds. Provisions shall be made by general law for the equitable distribution of such income among the several counties according to the number of children of school age in each; which several counties shall in like manner distribute the proportion of said fund by them received respectively to the several school districts embraced therein. But no appropriation shall be made from said fund to any district for the year in which a school has not been maintained for at least three months; nor shall any portion of any public school fund ever be used to support or assist any private school, or any school, academy, seminary, college or other institution of learning controlled by any church or sectarian organization or religious denomination whatsoever.

Sec. 12. Sectarianism prohibited. No sectarian instruction, qualifications or tests shall be imparted, exacted, applied or in any manner tolerated in the schools of any grade or character controlled by the state, nor shall attendance be required at any religious service therein, nor shall any sectarian tenets or doctrines be taught or favoured in any public school or institution that may be established under this constitution.

ARTICLE XV. TAXATION AND REVENUE

Sec. 12. Exemptions from taxation. The property of the United States, the State, counties, cities, towns, school districts and municipal corporations, when used primarily for a governmental purpose, and public libraries, lots with the buildings thereon used exclusively for religious worship, church parsonages, church schools and public cemeteries, shall be exempt from taxation, and such other property as the legislature may by general law provide.

ARTICLE XVI. PUBLIC INDEBTEDNESS

Sec. 6. Loan of credit; internal improvements. Neither the state nor any county, city, township, town, school district, or any other political subdivision shall loan or give its credit or make donations to or in aid of any individual, association or corporation, except for necessary support of the poor, nor subscribe to or become the owner of the capital stock of any association or corporation. . . .

ARTICLE XVII. STATE MILITIA

Sec. 1. Of whom constituted. The militia of the state shall consist of all able-bodied male citizens of the state, between the ages of eighteen and forty-five years; except such as are exempted by the law of the

United States or of the state. But all such citizens having scruples of conscience averse to bearing arms shall be excused therefrom upon such conditions as shall be prescribed by law.

ARTICLE XXI. SCHEDULE

Sec. 25. Religious liberty. Perfect toleration of religious sentiment shall be secured, and no inhabitant of this state shall ever be molested in person or property on account of his or her mode of religious worship.

Sec. 28. Provision for public schools. The legislature shall make laws for the establishment and maintenance of systems of public schools which shall be open to all the children of the state and free from sectarian control.

Table 1

RELIGIOUS GROUPS BY REGIONS

	% East	% Midwest	% South	% West
Baptist	12	21	58	9
Episcopal	41	14	22	23
Lutheran	19	55	10	16
Methodist	27	30	28	15
Presbyterian	29	28	25	18
Roman Catholic	41	28	16	15
Jewish	64	10	19	7

Table 2

RELIGIOUS GROUPS IN RURAL AREAS, TOWNS, AND CITIES

	% Rural– Small Town	% in Cities or Suburbs 50,000 to 1 Million Population	% in Cities Over 1,000,000 Population
Baptist	54	35	11
Episcopal	42	40	18
Lutheran	50	35	15
Methodist	58	31	11
Presbyterian	46	35	19
Roman Catholic	30	45	25
Jewish	12	34	54

Table 3

INCOME, 1975

	% Over $15,000	% $7,000 to $15,000	% Under $7,000
Episcopal	47	28	25
Jewish	47	25	28
Presbyterian	43	38	19
Lutheran	38	39	23
Roman Catholic	33	35	32
Methodist	31	40	29
Baptist	22	37	41

Table 4

OCCUPATION, 1975

	% Professional-Business	% Clerical-Sales	% Manual Workers	% Farmers
Jewish	46	15	13	0
Episcopal	37	15	22	2
Presbyterian	34	13	30	2
Methodist	23	11	37	2
Lutheran	21	16	36	5
Roman Catholic	20	13	44	2
Baptist	13	7	47	4

NOTE: 17% to 27% are not in the labor force. Thus total percentages will not add up to 100%.

Table 5

EDUCATION, 1975

	% College	% High School	% Grammar
Episcopal	54	36	10
Jewish	54	35	11
Presbyterian	41	51	8
Methodist	27	58	15
Roman Catholic	24	58	18
Lutheran	24	56	20
Baptist	16	57	27

Table 6

POLITICAL AFFILIATION, 1975

	% Democratic	% Republican	% Independent
Baptist	53	18	27
Episcopal	30	33	34
Jewish	59	8	32
Lutheran	30	29	38
Methodist	38	30	30
Presbyterian	30	39	30
Roman Catholic	52	14	31

Table 7

RELIGIOUS AFFILIATIONS IN CONGRESS, 1961–1977

	87th 1961-63	88th 1963-65	89th 1965-67	90th 1967-69	91st 1969-71	92nd 1971-73	93rd 1973-75	94th 1975-77
Baptist	66	63	55	55	52	49	55	57
Christian Science	4	3	3	4	4	5	5	4
Church of Christ	4	4	5	6	6	7	7	4
Disciples of Christ	16	13	12	12	13	14	9	5
Episcopal	66	64	68	67	66	68	66	65
Jewish	12	11	17	18	19	14	15	24
L.D.S. (Mormon)	7	8	10	9	10	10	10	10
Lutheran	22	17	17	13	14	14	16	14
Methodist	95	102	95	95	91	86	84	85
Presbyterian	73	82	75	81	80	83	78	66
Roman Catholic	99	99	109	109	112	113	115	124
Unitarian Universalist	7	10	14	8	6	8	9	13
United Church of Christ	26	25	24	29	29	27	27	24
"Protestant"	20	18	14	11	12	16	19	17

Table 8

RATIO OF RELIGIOUS CONGRESSIONAL REPRESENTATION

	% of Total Population	% of Congress 1975–77	Ratio
Baptist	13.8	10.7	.8
Episcopal	1.6	12.1	7.6
Jewish	3.0	4.5	1.5
L.D.S. (Mormon)	1.5	1.8	1.2
Lutheran	4.3	2.6	.6
Methodist	5.2	15.9	3.1
Presbyterian	2.1	12.3	5.9
Roman Catholic	22.9	23.2	1.0
Unitarian Universalist	.1	2.4	24.0
United Church of Christ	.9	4.5	5.0

The ratio is a measurement of the likelihood of Congressional representation for each religion. Unitarians, for example, are 24 times more likely to sit in Congress than their membership would indicate. Episcopalians are 8 times and Presbyterians 6 times more likely to do so. Baptists and Lutherans fail to attain adequate representation. The nonaffiliated are 38 times less likely to have a member of Congress.

Table 9

RELIGION AND PARTY AFFILIATION

	% Democratic 1961–63	% Democratic 1973–75	% Democratic 1975–77
Baptist	80.0	70.9	77.2
Episcopal	50.7	44.6	55.4
Jewish	83.3	80.0	83.3
L.D.S. (Mormon)	66.7	60.0	50.0
Lutheran	29.4	31.3	42.9
Methodist	61.7	53.6	64.7
Presbyterian	41.2	46.2	51.5
"Protestant"	52.6	57.9	88.2
Roman Catholic	82.8	71.0	79.8
Unitarian Universalist	57.1	66.7	76.9
United Church of Christ	19.2	44.4	58.3

Table 10

"LIBERAL QUOTIENT" BY RELIGION

	% Voting Liberal 94th Congress
Baptist	29.2
Episcopal	47.0
Jewish	76.7
L.D.S. (Mormon)	25.7
Lutheran	32.5
Methodist	36.7
Presbyterian	35.0
"Protestant"	73.9
Roman Catholic	64.7
Unitarian Universalist	74.2
United Church of Christ	65.1
Average for all	49.2

Table 11

PRAYER AMENDMENT VOTES

(1966 Dirksen and 1971 Wylie Amendments)

	% Yes
Baptist	72.3
Episcopal	53.6
Jewish	15.4
L.D.S. (Mormon)	28.6
Lutheran	82.8
Methodist	70.9
Presbyterian	70.4
"Protestant" or None	53.1
Roman Catholic	48.6
Unitarian Universalist	30.0
United Church of Christ	43.5
Average for all	59.2

Table 12
RELIGIOUS GROUPS BY COUNTIES

A. The 106 Heaviest Roman Catholic Counties

State	County
Arizona	Greenlee, Santa Cruz
Colorado	Conejos, Costilla
Connecticut	Windham
Illinois	Clinton
Indiana	Dubois
Iowa	Carroll, Dubuque, Howard
Louisiana	Acadia, Ascension, Assumption, Avoyelles, Cameron, Evangeline, Iberia, Jefferson, Jefferson Davis, Lafayette, Lafourche, Plaquemines, St. Bernard, St. Charles, St. James, St. John the Baptist, St. Landry, St. Martin, Terrebonne, Vermilion
Massachusetts	Bristol, Essex, Hampden, Norfolk, Plymouth, Suffolk, Worcester
Minnesota	Benton, Morrison, Red Lake, Scott, Stearns
Missouri	Osage, Perry, St. Genevieve
Montana	Blaine, Rosebud
Nebraska	Butler, Greeley
New Hampshire	Hillsboro
New Jersey	Hudson
New Mexico	Colfax, Guadalupe, Harding, Hidalgo, Mora, Rio Arriba, Sandoval, San Miguel, Santa Fe, Socorro, Taos, Torrance, Valencia
New York	Clinton, Franklin, Onondaga
North Dakota	Emmons, Morton, Rolette, Sioux, Stark
Ohio	Mercer, Putnam
Pennsylvania	Cambria, Elk, Lackawanna, Luzerne
Rhode Island	Bristol, Kent, Providence

110

South Dakota	Shannon, Washabaugh
Texas	Brooks, Cameron, Dimmit, Duval, Frio, Hidalgo, Hudspeth, Jeff Davis, La Salle, Lavaca, Maverick, Medina, Presidio, Starr, Webb, Willacy, Zapata, Zavala
Vermont	Grand Isle
Wisconsin	Brown, Iron, Kewaunee, Outagamie

B. The 96 Heaviest Baptist Counties

State	County
Alabama	Blount, Chilton, Clay, Cleburne, Cullman, St. Clair, Winston
Florida	Holmes, Lafayette
Georgia	Banks, Colquitt, Dawson, Dodge, Dooly, Fannin, Forsyth, Franklin, Gilmer, Glascock, Habersham, Haralson, Pulaski, Towns, Union, Wilcox
Kentucky	Ballard, Bell, Butler, Caldwell, Carlisle, Gallatin, Grant, Green, Hart, Knox, Larue, Logan, Mercer, Muhlenberg, Ohio, Owen, Shelby, Spencer, Trigg, Whitley
Louisiana	Grant, La Salle, Union, Winn
Mississippi	Calhoun, Lincoln, Lawrence, Pontotoc, Simpson, Smith, Union, Webster
North Carolina	Alexander, Cherokee, Clay, Cleveland, Graham, Jackson, Macon, Madison, Mitchell, Polk, Rutherford, Swain, Yancey
Oklahoma	Cotton, McClain, Tillman
South Carolina	Cherokee, Lee
Tennessee	Anderson, Claiborne, Grainger, Hancock, Hawkins, Jefferson, Loudon, McMinn, Meigs, Monroe, Polk, Sevier
Texas	Delta, Hall, Hardeman, Haskell, Hood, Schleicher, Stonewall, Throckmorton, Tyler

111

C. The 34 Heaviest Lutheran Counties

State	County
Iowa	Bremer, Winnebago, Worth
Minnesota	Big Stone, Chippewa, Fillmore, Freeborn, Goodhue, Grant, Jackson, Lac qui Parle, Lincoln, McLeod, Norman, Otter Tail, Pope, Sibley, Swift, Watonwan, Yellow Medicine
Nebraska	Dixon, Thayer
North Dakota	Bottineau, Griggs, Mercer, Nelson, Ransom, Renville, Sargent, Steele, Traill
South Dakota	Deuel, Hamlin
Wisconsin	Trempealeau

D. 50 Selected Evangelical Counties
(No One Denomination Predominates)

State	County
Arkansas	Greene, Jackson, Marion, Mississippi
Illinois	Union
Kentucky	Calloway, Livingston, Marshall, McCracken
Minnesota	Chisago, Kittson
Missouri	Dunklin, Greene, Carter, Reynolds, Texas
Nebraska	Burt
New Mexico	Roosevelt
Ohio	Adams, Ashland, Brown, Coshocton, Holmes, Wayne
Oklahoma	Bryan, Garvin, Harmon, Pushmataha
Pennsylvania	Adams, Bedford, Centre, Columbia, Cumberland, Franklin, Fulton, Greene, Juniata, Lycoming, Mifflin, Monroe, Montour, Perry, Snyder, Union, Wyoming, York
Tennessee	Chester, Crockett, Dyer, Madison

E. Selected Methodist Counties

State	County
Illinois	Pulaski
Kansas	Coffey, Comanche, Jewell, Kiowa, Lane, Ness, Stanton
Maryland	Caroline, Kent, Somerset
Nebraska	Deuel, Hitchcock, Hooker, Perkins
West Virginia	Morgan, Webster

F. Selected Yankee Protestant Counties

State	County
Illinois	Ford
Indiana	Jasper, Lagrange
Iowa	Story
Kansas	Douglas
Maine	Hancock, Lincoln
Massachusetts	Barnstable, Dukes, Nantucket
Michigan	Barry, Osceola
Missouri	Putnam
New Hampshire	Carroll
New York	Essex, Yates
Ohio	Geauga
Oregon	Benton
Pennsylvania	Tioga
South Dakota	Lawrence
Vermont	Lamoille, Orange
Wisconsin	Rock
(Boston	Ward 5)

INDEX

LEGAL ALMANAC SERIES CONVERSION TABLE
List of Original Titles and Authors

LEGAL ALMANAC SERIES CONVERSION TABLE
List of Present Titles and Authors